JODIE FOSTER

WOMEN of ACHIEVEMENT

JODIE FOSTER

Therese De Angelis

CHELSEA HOUSE PUBLISHERS
PHILADELPHIA

Frontis: *Jodie Foster in a relaxed mood. The star of such films as* Taxi Driver, The Silence of the Lambs, *and* Anna and the King, *Foster has made herself one of the most powerful women in Hollywood today.*

Cover Photos: Gregg DeGuire/London Features International, Ltd.

Chelsea House Publishers
EDITOR IN CHIEF Stephen Reginald
PRODUCTION MANAGER Pamela Loos
ART DIRECTOR Sara Davis
DIRECTOR OF PHOTOGRAPHY Judy L. Hasday
MANAGING EDITOR James D. Gallagher
SENIOR PRODUCTION EDITOR J. Christopher Higgins

Staff for **Jodie Foster**
ASSISTANT EDITOR Rob Quinn
ASSOCIATE ART DIRECTOR Takeshi Takahashi
DESIGNER/COVER DESIGNER Keith Trego
PICTURE RESEARCHER Judy L. Hasday

The Chelsea House World Wide Web address is:
http://www.chelseahouse.com

First Printing
1 3 5 7 9 8 6 4 2

Library of Congress Cataloging-in-Publication Data

De Angelis, Therese.
Jodie Foster / Therese De Angelis
  p.   cm.   — (Women of achievement)
Filmography: p.
Includes bibliographical references and index.
Summary: Discusses the personal life and professional career of the actress, producer, and director who has won an Academy Award for her roles in "Accused" and "The Silence of the Lambs."

ISBN 0-7910-5291-5 (hc) — ISBN 0-7910-5292-3 (pb)

1. Foster, Jodie—Juvenile literature. 2. Motion picture actors and actresses—United States—Biography—Juvenile literature. 3. Actresses—United States—Biography—Juvenile literature. 4. Motion picture producers and directors—United States—Biography—Juvenile literature. 5. 4. Women motion picture producers and directors—United States—Biography—Juvenile literature. [1. Foster, Jodie. 2. Actors and actresses. 3. Motion picture producers and directors. 4. Women—Biography.] I. Title. II. Series.
PN2287.F624 D43 2000
791.43'028'092—dc21
[B]   00-024301

CONTENTS

WOMEN of ACHIEVEMENT

Jane Addams
SOCIAL WORKER

Madeleine Albright
STATESWOMAN

Marian Anderson
SINGER

Susan B. Anthony
WOMAN SUFFRAGIST

Clara Barton
AMERICAN RED CROSS FOUNDER

Margaret Bourke-White
PHOTOGRAPHER

Rachel Carson
BIOLOGIST AND AUTHOR

Cher
SINGER AND ACTRESS

Hillary Rodham Clinton
FIRST LADY AND ATTORNEY

Katie Couric
JOURNALIST

Diana, Princess of Wales
HUMANITARIAN

Emily Dickinson
POET

Elizabeth Dole
POLITICIAN

Amelia Earhart
AVIATOR

Gloria Estefan
SINGER

Jodie Foster
ACTRESS AND DIRECTOR

Betty Friedan
FEMINIST

Althea Gibson
TENNIS CHAMPION

Ruth Bader Ginsburg
SUPREME COURT JUSTICE

Helen Hayes
ACTRESS

Katharine Hepburn
ACTRESS

Mahalia Jackson
GOSPEL SINGER

Helen Keller
HUMANITARIAN

**Ann Landers/
Abigail Van Buren**
COLUMNISTS

Barbara McClintock
BIOLOGIST

Margaret Mead
ANTHROPOLOGIST

Edna St. Vincent Millay
POET

Julia Morgan
ARCHITECT

Toni Morrison
AUTHOR

Grandma Moses
PAINTER

Lucretia Mott
WOMAN SUFFRAGIST

Sandra Day O'Connor
SUPREME COURT JUSTICE

Rosie O'Donnell
ENTERTAINER AND COMEDIAN

Georgia O'Keeffe
PAINTER

Eleanor Roosevelt
DIPLOMAT AND HUMANITARIAN

Wilma Rudolph
CHAMPION ATHLETE

Elizabeth Cady Stanton
WOMAN SUFFRAGIST

Harriet Beecher Stowe
AUTHOR AND ABOLITIONIST

Barbra Streisand
ENTERTAINER

Elizabeth Taylor
ACTRESS AND ACTIVIST

Mother Teresa
HUMANITARIAN AND
RELIGIOUS LEADER

Barbara Walters
JOURNALIST

Edith Wharton
AUTHOR

Phillis Wheatley
POET

Oprah Winfrey
ENTERTAINER

Babe Didrikson Zaharias
CHAMPION ATHLETE

"REMEMBER THE LADIES"

MATINA S. HORNER

"Remember the Ladies." That is what Abigail Adams wrote to her husband John, then a delegate to the Continental Congress, as the Founding Fathers met in Philadelphia to form a new nation in March of 1776. "Be more generous and favorable to them than your ancestors. Do not put such unlimited power in the hands of the Husbands. If particular care and attention is not paid to the Ladies," Abigail Adams warned, "we are determined to foment a Rebellion, and will not hold ourselves bound by any Laws in which we have no voice, or Representation."

The words of Abigail Adams, one of the earliest American advocates of women's rights, were prophetic. Because when we have not "remembered the ladies," they have, by their words and deeds, reminded us so forcefully of the omission that we cannot fail to remember them. For the history of American women is as interesting and varied as the history of our nation as a whole. American women have played an integral part in founding, settling, and building our country. Some we remember as remarkable women who—against great odds—achieved distinction in the public arena: Anne Hutchinson, who in the 17th century became a charismatic religious leader; Phillis Wheatley, an 18th-century black slave who became a poet; Susan B. Anthony, whose name is synonymous with the 19th-century women's rights movement, and who led the struggle to enfranchise women; and in the 20th century, Amelia Earhart, the first woman to cross the Atlantic Ocean by air.

These extraordinary women certainly merit our admiration, but other women, "common women," many of them all but forgotten, should also be recognized for their contributions to American thought and culture. Women have been community builders; they have founded schools and formed voluntary associations to help those in need; they have assumed the major responsibility for rearing children, passing on from one generation to the next the values that keep a culture alive. These and innumerable other contributions, once ignored, are now being recognized by scholars, students, and the public. It is exciting and gratifying that a part of our history that was hardly acknowledged a few generations ago is now being studied and brought to light.

In recent decades, the field of women's history has grown from obscurity to a politically controversial splinter movement to academic respectability, in many cases mainstreamed into such traditional disciplines as history, economics, and psychology. Scholars of women, both female and male, have organized research centers at such prestigious institutions as Wellesley College, Stanford University, and the University of California. Other notable centers for women's studies are the Center for the American Woman and Politics at the Eagleton Institute of Politics at Rutgers University; the Henry A. Murray Research Center for the Study of Lives, at Radcliffe College; and the Women's Research and Education Institute, the research arm of the Congressional Caucus on Women's Issues. Other scholars and public figures have established archives and libraries, such as the Schlesinger Library on the History of Women in America, at Radcliffe College, and the Sophia Smith Collection, at Smith College, to collect and preserve the written and tangible legacies of women.

From the initial donation of the Women's Rights Collection in 1943, the Schlesinger Library grew to encompass vast collections documenting the manifold accomplishments of American women. Simultaneously, the women's movement in general and the academic discipline of women's studies in particular also began with a narrow definition and gradually expanded their mandate. Early causes, such as woman suffrage and social reform, abolition, and organized labor were joined by newer concerns, such as the history of women in business and the professions and in politics and government; the study of the family; and social issues such as health policy and education.

Women, as historian Arthur M. Schlesinger, jr., once pointed out, "have constituted the most spectacular casualty of traditional history. They have made up at least half the human race, but you could never tell that by looking at the books historians write." The new breed of historians is remedying that omission. They have written books about immigrant women and about working-class women who struggled for survival in cities and about black women who met the challenges of life in rural areas. They are telling the stories of women who, despite the barriers of tradition and economics, became lawyers and doctors and public figures.

The women's studies movement has also led scholars to question traditional interpretations of their respective disciplines. For example, the study of war has traditionally been an exercise in military and political analysis, an examination of strategies planned and executed by men. But scholars of women's history have pointed out that wars have also been periods of tremendous change and even opportunity for women, because the very absence of men on the home front enabled them to expand their educational, economic, and professional activities and to assume leadership in their homes.

The early scholars of women's history showed a unique brand of courage in choosing to investigate new subjects and take new approaches to old ones. Often, like their subjects, they endured criticism and even ostracism by their academic colleagues. But their efforts have unquestionably been worthwhile, because with the publication of each new study and book another piece of the historical patchwork is sewn into place, revealing an increasingly comprehensive picture of the role of women in our rich and varied history.

Such books on groups of women are essential, but books that focus on the lives of individuals are equally indispensable. Biographies can be inspirational, offering their readers the example of people with vision who have looked outside themselves for their goals and have often struggled against great obstacles to achieve them. Marian Anderson, for instance, had to overcome racial bigotry in order to perfect her art and perform as a concert singer. Isadora Duncan defied the rules of classical dance to find true artistic freedom. Jane Addams had to break down society's notions of the proper role for women in order to create new social situations, notably the settlement house. All of these women had to come to terms both with themselves and with the world in which they lived. Only then could they move ahead as pioneers in their chosen callings.

Biography can inspire not only by adulation but also by realism. It helps us to see not only the qualities in others that we hope to emulate, but also, perhaps, the weaknesses that made them "human." By helping us identify with the subject on a more personal level they help us feel that we, too, can achieve such goals. We read about Eleanor Roosevelt, for instance, who occupied a unique and seemingly enviable position as the wife of the president. Yet we can sympathize with her inner dilemma; an inherently shy woman, she had to force herself to live a most public life in order to use her position to benefit others. We may not be able to imagine ourselves having the immense poetic talent of Emily Dickinson, but from her story we can understand the challenges faced by a creative woman who was expected to fulfill many family responsibilities. And though few of us will ever reach the level of athletic accomplishment displayed by Wilma Rudolph or Babe Zaharias, we can still appreciate their spirit, their overwhelming will to excel.

A biography is a multifaceted lens. It is first of all a magnification, the intimate examination of one particular life. But at the same time, it is a wide-angle lens, informing us about the world in which the subject lived. We come away from reading about one life knowing more about the social, political, and economic fabric of the time. It is for this reason, perhaps, that the great New England essayist Ralph Waldo Emerson wrote in 1841, "There is properly no history: only biography." And it is also why biography, and particularly women's biography, will continue to fascinate writers and readers alike.

Jodie Foster proudly shows off the Oscar she won in 1989 for her role in The Accused. *She beat out such notable actresses as Glenn Close* (Dangerous Liaisons), *Melanie Griffith* (Working Girl), *Meryl Streep* (Ironweed), *and Sigourney Weaver* (Gorillas in the Mist) *for the coveted Academy Award.*

1

"MY LIFE IS SO SIMPLE"

odie Foster was in the midst of a three-week European tour to promote her new film, *The Accused*, when the Academy of Motion Picture Arts and Sciences announced its Oscar nominees for 1988. The 26-year-old actress, who was boarding a plane in Rome, Italy, learned that she was one of five women nominated for Best Actress, along with Glenn Close, Melanie Griffith, Meryl Streep, and Sigourney Weaver. "A man from [the airline] Alitalia came right out on the tarmac and the people on the plane clapped for me," Foster remembered later.

But Foster had a difficult time believing that her role in *The Accused* could have earned her an Oscar nomination. After filming ended, she had felt so unsure of her performance that she seriously considered giving up acting and returning to school. "I was gonna go to Cornell and be a grad student in literature, and no one would ever hear from me again. I'd be found out as a fraud," she told *Entertainment Weekly* years later. "The film was just very provocative for me personally."

The Accused is based on the true story of a young woman who was repeatedly raped at knifepoint in a New Bedford, Massachu-

Filming this solitary dance sequence in the bar "was definitely the hardest scene in the movie for me," Foster admitted later. The actress had to seem oblivious to everything that was going on around her, when in fact she knew what was to come—a brutal rape scene.

setts, bar in March 1983 while several drunk onlookers cheered on the attackers. In real life four of the six men who were arrested for the rape were jailed; the other two, who allegedly held the woman down, were acquitted. Filming such a disturbing event was emotionally exhausting not only for Foster, who plays rape victim Sarah Tobias in the movie, but also for the rest of the cast. Many of them broke down in tears after several takes. Some crew members complained to director Jonathan Kaplan that they were losing sleep over the scene, which took five days to shoot. The normally unruffled actress immersed herself in the role so deeply that she grew moody and found herself snapping at her friends. She later admitted that she also suffered panic attacks over performing in the rape scene.

More challenging for Foster, however, was another scene in which her character, who has been drinking, dances suggestively in the bar just minutes before she is attacked. "That was definitely the hardest scene in the movie for me," she told an interviewer in 1991. "Obviously, no one else is dancing, there's no music on [because the sound track was added later]. I wanted it to be completely unhesitating. And it's a hard thing to do when you know what's going to happen later."

Why take on such an intense, difficult role? Jodie Foster saw Sarah Tobias not as a powerless victim but as a personification of the humiliation and outrage that plague women who have been raped. Foster also wanted to tell the story of a person who summons the courage to fight for herself. "I wanted Sarah to be able to prove herself, to be a good witness, to find her own voice, to prove to society that she could rise above their low expectations of her. If I did that, I'll be happy," she said.

In describing her portrayal of Sarah Tobias, Jodie Foster might well have been speaking about her own life. A former child star who began acting in commercials at the age of three, Foster is very familiar not only with Hollywood but also with the pressures of being a celebrity. And she has weathered several crises that might have defeated a less determined or less professional actress. When she was eight years old, she was mauled by a lion while filming the Disney movie *Napoleon and Samantha*, but she returned to complete the filming less than two weeks later. At 13 she earned her first Academy Award nomination by playing a prostitute in the controversial film *Taxi Driver*. And in 1981 the Yale University student became the center of a media storm when a man named John Hinckley Jr. attempted to assassinate President Ronald Reagan, then claimed he had done it solely to win Jodie's affection.

But Jodie Foster has survived, navigating almost

effortlessly the difficult transition from child star to adult actress. Today she commands $15 million per film role, a salary unmatched by any actress except Julia Roberts.

Business associates, friends, and family members attribute Jodie's success not only to her talent and intelligence but also to her toughness and self-discipline. While still a toddler she became the Foster family's main source of income. Her divorced mother, Brandy, began taking her two youngest children to television auditions to earn money for the family without having to leave her children alone every day. "I think there's a turbulence in Jodie that comes from being the bread-earner . . . in the family," *Nell* costar Liam Neeson said of her in 1995. Jodie herself admits that growing up on movie and television sets forced her to develop self-restraint. "When I was a kid I just didn't think I was allowed to say no. I didn't think I was allowed to complain," she said years later. "I guess I thought I'd get fired or they'd be mad at me."

But when Jodie Foster was announced as the winner of the 1988 Oscar for Best Actress for her performance in *The Accused*, she credited her achievement to the strong and supportive people in her life—her family and coworkers, the people who had helped her reach the pinnacle of her acting career, and especially her mother. Foster took the stage to accept her award and delivered a brief but moving speech:

> This is such a big deal and my life is so simple. There are very few [important] things—there's love and work and family. And this movie is so special to us because it was all three of those things. And I'd like to thank all of my families, the tribes that I come from, the wonderful crew on *The Accused*, Jonathan Kaplan, Kelly McGillis, Tom Topor, Paramount [Pictures], the Academy, my schools . . . and most importantly my mother, Brandy, who taught me that all my finger paintings were Picassos and that I didn't have to be afraid. And mostly that cruelty might be very human

and it might be very cultural but it's not acceptable, which is what this movie is all about. Thank you so much.

Backstage after the awards, Jodie declared that her golden Oscar statuette was going to open doors for her—at the local video store. "I rented three videos last night . . . and they said if I brought this in I would get them free. So you can bet this is going back to the store tomorrow," she joked.

Clearly, for Jodie Foster the simple life she had spoken about only moments before was not just a cliché. For the wildly successful actress, maintaining a low public profile and leading a private life are as important as achieving professional recognition. An old friend and former Yale classmate of Foster's says, "I think she would do anything to remain inconspicuous for the rest of her life."

Foster's desire for privacy became even stronger in July 1998, when she gave birth to a son, Charles. The former child star, who was herself raised by a single mother, is concerned but optimistic about raising her son alone in the nearly constant glare of media attention. "You just try to be as healthy as possible," she said a month after Charles's birth. "I can't say being a celebrity is a great thing; there's nothing good about it besides the work. . . . The rest of it, the lack of anonymity, there's just nothing fun about it. It will just be another obstacle [Charles] will have. I have to think about how to minimize the damage."

That outlook—cautious but determined—has allowed Jodie Foster to forge a path as a respected film director and producer in a business where very few women have been able to achieve the recognition or financial backing to do so. And she has managed to do all of this in a successful career that has run longer than those of many Hollywood stars twice her age.

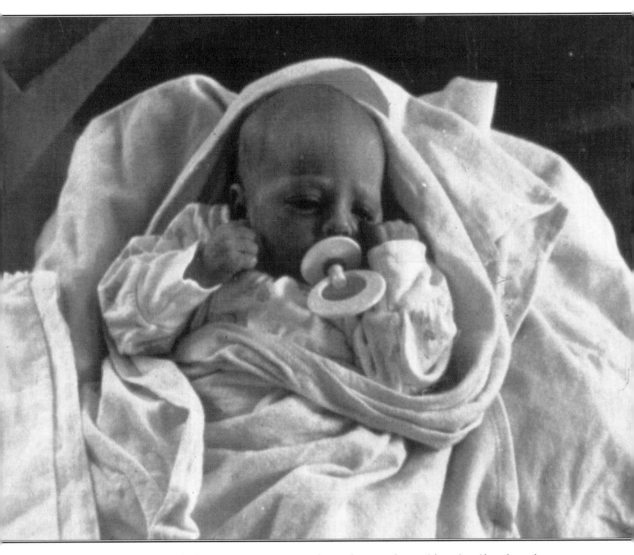

Alicia Christian "Jodie" Foster was a star only to the members of her family when she was born on November 19, 1962—but that would change within a few years.

2

THE BREADWINNER

By the time Alicia Christian Foster was born in Los Angeles, California, on November 19, 1962, her parents had separated. "Jodie," as she was nicknamed early on, was the fourth child of Evelyn "Brandy" Foster and Lucius Fisher Foster III, a U.S. Air Force officer. Although Brandy had filed for divorce three years earlier, the couple had struggled to stay together. But their relationship had grown increasingly bitter and turbulent until, just months before Jodie's birth, Lucius left his family for good.

Brandy Foster's childhood had been difficult. She was born Evelyn Della Almond in the Bronx, New York, on September 21, 1928, to a young, unmarried Irish woman named Josie Almond. Josie had become pregnant by a German businessman with whom she had been conducting a secret affair. Shamed by Josie's condition, her parents sequestered their daughter in the house during her pregnancy, claiming that she was suffering from a lengthy illness. Shortly after Evelyn was born, the Almonds took the infant to Rockford, Illinois, to be raised by a cousin, John Almond, and his wife, Lucy Lefler Almond.

With no children of their own, John and Lucy took their child-rearing responsibilities very seriously. A devout churchgoer, Lucy proved an affectionate but stern parent. She insisted that Evelyn adhere to strict rules of etiquette and punished her for the slightest offenses. But Evelyn was a rambunctious and defiant child. One day the toddler discovered the Almonds' supply of brandy, which they kept on hand for medicinal purposes. After consuming a considerable amount of the alcohol, she wandered into another room and, in front of the astonished adults, danced a jig and then fell asleep. The Almonds were so amused by the child's performance that they decided not to punish her. Instead they nicknamed her "Brandy."

After the United States entered World War II, Rockford became a reception center for U.S. Army recruits, and the town filled with soldiers preparing to ship overseas. With so many new and handsome young men in town, Brandy, now a precocious and attractive teen, proved more difficult than ever to discipline. At the same time, the Almonds' marriage began to disintegrate. Brandy learned that John was having an affair with a next-door neighbor when she saw the two adults signaling each other from the windows of their homes. Lucy did not learn about her husband's unfaithfulness, however, until he abandoned them and left town with the neighbor.

Fortunately, other members of the Almond family agreed to take in Lucy and Brandy until Lucy could find a job. She eventually found work as a forewoman for the Barber Coleman Company, a manufacturer of machine tools. There Lucy met a machinist named Charles Schmidt, and they were married soon after.

Charles, who was described years later by a friend of Lucy's as a "loving and gentle man," was nonetheless shocked at his stepdaughter's wild behavior. After a scandalous incident in the summer of 1942—in which Brandy was discovered making out with an army

recruit in the back seat of a car—Charles enrolled her in St. Mary's Academy, a Catholic high school for girls in Milwaukee, Wisconsin. Angry over being sent away from home and forced to endure the rigorous training of St. Mary's, Brandy grew resentful toward Lucy and Charles. She vowed that after she graduated, she would leave Rockford behind for good.

Brandy's first destination was Chicago, Illinois, where she landed a job as a singer in the city's jazz clubs. She fell in love with and married a young navy man, but the marriage was brief. After her divorce she and a friend, Gloria Cannon, decided to make a fresh start by driving to the glamorous city of Los Angeles.

In the book *Foster Child*, Brandy's son Buddy Foster says that his mother took an administrative position with the Bell Telephone division that published the

Jodie's mother, Evelyn "Brandy" Foster (left), and her father, Lucius Foster III (right), were in the process of ending their eight-year marriage when their fourth child was born in 1962.

city's Yellow Pages before meeting the man who would become her husband, Lucius Foster III. Another source claims that she was a buyer of baby clothes for a downtown department store. Whatever Brandy's job experience was, one fact was certain: when she and the dashing lieutenant colonel met, it was a case of love at first sight. "[Brandy] was the most beautiful woman I had ever met," Lucius Foster admitted years after their divorce. "She was articulate, outspoken, everything I had ever wanted in a woman."

Lucius Foster III had been born on April 16, 1922. He was the only child of strong-willed—and alcoholic—parents, Lucius II and Constance Foster. Eventually Lucius II became sober, but he left his wife and young son, and when he remarried a few years later he lost contact with them. Left alone with his mother, Lucius III endured her frequent drinking binges, violent outbursts, and bouts of deep depression. One day the youngster was a passenger in Constance's car when she drunkenly barreled head-on into a Model T and drove off, leaving the other car in pieces and the driver to fend for himself. When the police arrived at her house the following morning, Constance exhibited no remorse. "I was far too drunk last night to recall any such accident," she snapped. Her generous monetary gifts to policemen's charities may have been the reason she was given only a warning for her reckless behavior.

Despite her drinking problem, Constance managed to found a world-renowned sportswear business, and the profits from her company allowed her to purchase an elegant mansion in Beverly Hills, California. She was also a skilled pilot—one of very few women in the country at that time who knew how to fly—and from her Lucius III developed his love of flying. At New York University he studied engineering and aeronautics, and when World War II broke out in 1939, he was so eager to join the fighting that he traveled to Canada, where he enrolled in the Royal Canadian Air Force (the

United States would not enter the war until 1941). Later he was granted amnesty by the United States for abandoning his citizenship, and he earned a commission with the U.S. Army Eighth Air Force. He continued to fly war missions over Europe and the Pacific, earning several combat decorations.

When Brandy met Lucius, he already had three sons by a previous marriage, but the fact that he had little contact with them did not seem to bother her. In 1954, during a romantic New Year's weekend in Tijuana, Mexico, Brandy Almond and Lucius Fisher Foster III were married. Their first child, Lucinda ("Cindy"), was born later that year. The following year Constance ("Connie") was born, and in 1957 Brandy gave birth to Lucius Fisher IV, later nicknamed "Buddy." They settled in a 1930s Spanish-style home in Laurel Canyon, overlooking Los Angeles.

The marriage was troubled from the start. Lucius was a womanizer, and his almost constant affairs were the subject of fierce battles between him and his wife. After such arguments, he would usually storm out of the house and stay away for days at a time. Finally Brandy had had enough. She filed for divorce when Buddy was two years old, and although she became pregnant with Jodie during a brief reconciliation with Lucius, their bitter quarrels over alimony payments and the division of their possessions resumed soon after.

After the divorce became final, Brandy and her three children moved from the spacious house in Laurel Canyon into a cramped duplex in an area called "the Flats." Brandy was receiving several hundred dollars a month in alimony, but even with her part-time job as a press agent she knew that she would need much more to raise her family on her own, especially with another child on the way.

At work she became friendly with several other women who were divorced or separated and who sympathized with her plight. One of them, Josephine Hill, had recently purchased a large house in the middle of an orange grove in the San Fernando Valley, and she invited Brandy to live with her and her son, Chris. Brandy readily accepted the invitation and moved in six months after Jodie was born. The women and their children quickly formed a makeshift family. Before long, Brandy's children were calling their mother's friend "Aunt Jo."

By all accounts Jodie was an extremely precocious child. Her brother claims that she was walking when she was only seven months old; her mother says that Jodie began to talk at nine months and was reading when she was three years old. "One day we were driving along and she began reading billboard signs aloud to me," Brandy said. "I thought she had memorized what her older sister had taught her. I soon found out, much to my amazement, that she could read."

Engaging and easygoing, Jodie nonetheless had a strong personality even as a toddler. Her brother remembers her as somewhat of an escape artist—skilled at slipping through gates, locks, and windows—and as a fearless and curious child. "Once I captured a snake and showed Jodie the angry, hissing serpent up close, thinking it would convince her not to follow us anymore," he relates in his book. "But it had the opposite effect: she was fascinated and wanted to hold it."

Even with the help of Josephine Hill, Brandy Foster's financial situation became even more precarious after Jodie was born. The solution to her troubles came from an unexpected source. One of Josephine's neighbors had an eight-year-old son, Greg, who had appeared in several television commercials. "He bragged that he had bought himself a cool minibike and already had money saved for college," Buddy recalls in *Foster Child*. "There was no doubt in my mind I could do as well— and better."

After researching acting agencies, Brandy discovered Toni Kelman, a woman who had established her own

business. Buddy, a handsome blond boy with sparkling blue eyes and an easy smile, was a hit with ad agency representatives. He began filming TV commercial spots advertising products such as Kellogg's cereal and Mattel toys. Before long he was earning about $25,000 a year.

With the income from Buddy's acting jobs, Brandy was able to move her family into their own home. She purchased a run-down but charming mission-style house in Hollywood. It was a practical location, considering Buddy's work and her new job as a film publicist for producer Arthur Jacobs. By indulging in her love of antiques, Brandy managed to turn the house into a tasteful and interesting home. Years later Jodie Foster fondly remembered her mother's flair for creating a warm and inviting atmosphere: "We didn't have much, but what we had was exquisite. . . . We always had good Tuscan bread around and my mother drove a

Toddler Jodie with her older brother, Buddy Foster, and Chris Hill, the son of a family friend. Josephine Hill, Chris's mother, invited Brandy Foster and her children to live with her and her son after Brandy's marriage ended. Six months after Jodie was born, Brandy accepted the offer.

Five-year-old Jodie in a commercial for Crest toothpaste. Buddy Foster was already established as a commercial actor when Jodie was spotted at an audition and invited to give acting a try.

Peugeot and she took us to arty movies. . . . We had beautiful furniture and leatherbound books in different languages," she said. Jodie also recalled one of her mother's ingenious methods for coming up with extra cash on short notice. "My mother collects chairs. . . . So every time we became poor . . . she'd just sell [one of] the chairs."

One day Brandy found herself without a baby-sitter for three-year-old Jodie, so she took her along to one of Buddy's auditions. Buddy was trying out for a part in a Coppertone suntan lotion commercial, but the boy's audition had hardly begun before Coppertone executives had their eye on the little girl Brandy had in tow. "When they told him to take off his shirt, I was behind him," Jodie told *Interview* magazine in 1991, "and I took off my shirt, too, and did my muscles like he did—because I loved my brother. They said, 'What's your name, little girl?'" In the end Jodie, not Buddy,

got the part. Jodie became the TV version of Coppertone's famous print image: a blond, tanned toddler
showing a pale bottom as a puppy tugs at her swimsuit.

Before long Jodie was as much in demand as her
brother was. Over the next two years, she appeared in
scores of TV commercials advertising products like
Oreo cookies, Ken-L Ration dog food, and Crest
toothpaste. In 1974 the 12-year-old vividly described
her memories of shooting and reshooting commercials:
"I remember . . . doing them over and over again, having to eat sickening things all day and throwing up.
After being in a shampoo ad I couldn't get the [stuff]
out of my hair for ten days."

Although the job sounds unappealing at best, Jodie
now insists that she had a great time as a child actor and
wouldn't have wanted to grow up any differently. In
fact, she says, it afforded her a unique opportunity that
most kids never have. "Most kids, all they have is
school," Foster told *Time* magazine in 1991. "I [had]
my work; I [knew] how to talk to adults and how to
make a decision. Acting . . . spared me from being a
regular everyday kid slob."

The year Jodie landed the Coppertone job, Brandy
took the advice of show-business colleagues and began
seeking acting parts for Buddy in television shows. His
first costarring role was in a series called *Hondo*, an
ABC western. The show lasted less than one season,
but Buddy was soon tapped for another TV role, as
actor Ken Berry's son in CBS's *Mayberry, R.F.D.*, a
spin-off of the long-running *Andy Griffith Show. Mayberry, R.F.D.*, which premiered in the fall of 1968,
turned out to be lucrative for the Foster family. Not
only did it run for four seasons, providing Buddy with
a steady job, but it would also give Jodie—already a
veteran actress at six years old—the opportunity to
break out of television commercials and into more sub-
stantial roles.

Twelve-year-old Jodie, in a relaxed mode during an interview.

3

CHILD STAR

Jodie Foster had barely reached school age when in 1969 she earned a part in an episode of *Mayberry, R.F.D.*, the television series in which Buddy was already a regular. Her part was relatively small—she portrayed a ballerina and was on-screen for just a few minutes—but it was an important stepping-stone in what would become her lifelong career. "I remember [it as] being a big deal," Jodie told an interviewer years later. "I had a long feather boa and a tiara and little sequined shorts, and I remember . . . seeing my family out there, beaming from ear to ear."

Jodie must have impressed more than family members: the following year she earned her own regular role as a recurring character on the comedy series *The Courtship of Eddie's Father*, which starred Bill Bixby as the widowed father of a boy played by Brandon Cruz. Jodie played Joey Kelly, a tomboyish seven-year-old who keeps house and takes care of her own single dad. The show ran for two years, but by the time it was canceled in 1972 Jodie had also appeared in several episodes of the popular TV westerns *Gunsmoke* and *Bonanza*, the drama *Ironside*, and other programs, including *Julia* and *Ghost Story*. She also had the title role in a pilot called *My*

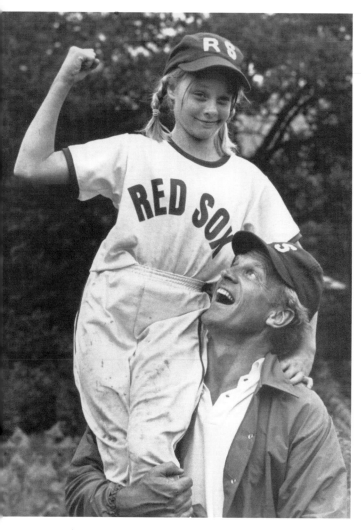

Jodie Foster and Ned Wilson in a shot from the ABC Afterschool Special "Rookie of the Year."

Sister Hank (the series was never aired), and in an ABC *Afterschool Special* called "Rookie of the Year" she played a girl who breaks the gender barrier to join her town's Little League team. The TV movie later won an Emmy Award.

With two child actors in the family, Brandy Foster had a hectic schedule. Josephine Hill often baby-sat the other Foster children while Brandy, who had her own career, drove Buddy and Jodie to and from their acting jobs. Although the two youngsters were now fairly well known on television, Brandy constantly reminded them that what they were doing was simply a job and that they were no different from other kids their age. She was purposefully strict with her children, she related years later, because she believed in providing them with a strong role model who would not "break down" under pressure. "All of us were in it together," Jodie has said of her family during those years. "My mom worked, we all did. Just to survive."

Brandy not only instilled a strong work ethic in her children, but she also exposed them to a rich cultural environment. In addition to the antiques she collected and displayed, she also introduced her children to exotic cuisines—Russian, Portuguese, Korean, Thai, Vietnamese, and Philippine dishes were often on the Foster menu—and to her own love for foreign films, especially French cinema. As a child, Jodie told an interviewer in 1991, "I spent my whole life going to see very dark

European films" because her mother enjoyed them and wanted to share the films with her. Such mutual interests created a strong bond between mother and daughter that remains today.

Although Jodie worked hard and kept up on her household responsibilities, her schoolwork did not seem to be a chore for her. An exceptionally bright child, Jodie was tested for California's gifted program when she was in third grade. Her results were so good that school officials urged Brandy to allow Jodie to skip the fourth grade. They also suggested that she encourage her daughter to pursue science. "I didn't want her skipped," Brandy recalled in a 1988 interview, "[and] I wanted her challenge to be in another language." After Brandy did some research, she decided to enroll her daughter in Le Lycée Français, an exclusive private school in Los Angeles known for its rigorous discipline and emphasis on the classics.

Jodie attended the lycée until she received her high school diploma. According to law, child actors are required to receive schooling even while they are on a set or on location, so Jodie learned at an early age how to juggle schoolwork and acting—and she did both very well. "I would do 20 minutes of math, then be called to the set to do a scene, then do 40 minutes of English, then be called back to the set," Jodie recalls. "I learned how to have an immediate sense of concentration." John Badham, who later directed hit films such as *Saturday Night Fever* and *Stakeout*, agrees. He remembers directing Jodie Foster in an episode of the TV series *Kung Fu*. Even at 10 years old, "Jodie's attention never wavered and she was never distracted by the long days, the tedium, or the take-after-take repetition," Badham says. "She was just right there, just whatever was needed. . . . She had a quiet charisma, and it came through whether on-camera or off-camera. You felt like you were in the presence of an adult."

The same year that Jodie nearly got her own TV

Brandy Foster believed that Jodie's education was as important as her work. She enrolled her youngest daughter in Le Lycée Français de Los Angeles, an exclusive private school.

series, Buddy lost his job on *Mayberry, R.F.D.* when the network announced that it was canceling the show. Brandy began to realize that the best and most lucrative acting jobs for children were in motion pictures. She had already raised Jodie's asking price from the standard rate of $450 a week to $1,000, and now she also began auditioning her daughter for feature films.

It wasn't long before Jodie earned a movie role. In 1972 she began filming the Disney adventure *Napoleon and Samantha*, a story about an orphaned boy who runs away with an elderly circus lion named Major and takes refuge with a reclusive college student (played by a 20-year-old actor named Michael Douglas). Jodie played Samantha opposite child star Johnny Whitaker, who also had a starring role in the hit TV series *Family Affair*.

But Jodie's movie career nearly ended before it began. While on location in Oregon, she was mauled by one of the lions trained to work with the two young actors. As a teenager, Jodie recalled the incident:

> There were two lions—one who was a stand-in, named Zambo, and another who was 25 years old, named Major, who had all his teeth out and couldn't do anything [dangerous].
>
> It was really hot, like four o'clock in the afternoon, and you're not supposed to work lions after three. And Major wouldn't do [the scene], so they got Zambo to do it.
>
> Finally we got the shot. I was walking up the hill and the lion was behind me, being pulled by a piano wire—that was the only way they could get him to go. And I wasn't walking fast enough. He came around and bit me.

In another interview 20 years later the actress provided more vivid details about the terrifying incident. The lion "picked me up in his mouth and shook me around like a rabbit," she recalled. "I thought it was an earthquake because I came from L.A. . . . I watched everybody run away. . . . Then the trainer said, 'Drop it!' [to the lion] and I went rolling down a hill. It was pretty dramatic." Jodie was quickly flown to a hospital in Portland. She received a series of shots and the puncture wounds she sustained—both front and back—were closed with several stitches.

Ten days later the plucky youngster was back on the set. Her mother had allowed her to make her own decision about whether to finish the movie, "but I think she felt it was smarter for me to go back, you know, to get back on the horse that bucked me," Jodie explained.

By the time *Napoleon and Samantha* premiered in theaters, Jodie Foster was hard at work on several other projects, both in television and on film. In the same year, she played the daughter of a Roller Derby queen (Raquel Welch) in the unsuccessful movie *Kansas City Bomber*, and over the next few years her small-screen appearances included roles on *The Partridge Family*,

Medical Center, Love Story, and the TV version of the movie *Bob and Carol and Ted and Alice*. In 1973 she appeared in two feature films: *One Little Indian*, an Old West story starring James Garner, and a musical version of *Tom Sawyer*, in which she costarred as Becky Thatcher, once more opposite Johnny Whitaker. At the 1974 Academy Awards ceremony, the two pint-size stars performed an Oscar-nominated song from the Disney animated movie *Robin Hood* to a charmed audience.

Around this time Jodie was also tapped to play another tough kid, this time in a television series based on the 1973 movie *Paper Moon*, which had costarred actress Tatum O'Neal and her father, Ryan. Tatum had won a Best Supporting Actress Oscar for her performance as Addie Pray. In the TV version Jodie played Addie, and at 11 years old she felt the pressure of living up to another actress's award-winning performance. Though she enjoyed filming the series, which was shot in a small Kansas town during the summer of 1974, she complained that because of the short haircut she sported for the role, the town's residents were constantly mistaking her for a boy. Even worse, she told one interviewer, was the fact that "everyone thinks I should look like Tatum O'Neal." Despite Jodie's talent, *Paper Moon* was canceled before the season ended, and Brandy Foster redoubled her efforts to find appropriate film roles for her daughter.

Not yet a teenager, Jodie was earning critical attention that actors three times her age would have longed for. She received favorable reviews for *Tom Sawyer*: the *Hollywood Reporter* called her "refreshing," adding that "she looks sweet but she's a very feisty kid." *Time* magazine praised Jodie's down-to-earth performance, declaring that "only Jodie Foster, as Becky, suggests that she somehow remembers what it is like to be a real person in a real world." And when she was compared to Hollywood's most renowned child star, Shirley Temple, Jodie showed a precocious sense of her own place in the

world of acting: "I still play a sweet little kid," she said. "It's just that my sweet little kid is modernized. The Shirley Temple kid doesn't sell anymore. But I don't think I'm so different from her. I think that kids always have been smarter than adults think they are. Maybe the difference with me is that my characters show that a little more."

The youngster's insightful observations could not obscure the fact that, at heart, she was still a child with child-size ambitions. In September 1974 she listed her four greatest goals for a Los Angeles newspaper reporter: "I want to be president of the United States," she told the interviewer. "I want to go on the stage. I want to go to Rome. And I want to get a hamster."

While Jodie was flourishing as an actress, her brother was floundering. Now 16, Buddy Foster was growing increasingly resentful and defiant about performing,

Despite being chomped by a lion during the filming of Disney's Napoleon and Samantha, *Jodie was back on the set within 10 days. Here, she is pictured with a relaxed lion and with costar Johnny Whitaker.*

Jodie takes a leap in front of the family home. Buddy and Jodie's successful acting careers enabled their mother to move the family out of friend Josephine Hill's home and into a house in a new neighborhood.

and he began to long for a different kind of life, a "normal" life. "The seeds of rebellion were growing in me," he relates in *Foster Child*. "I wanted . . . to be like the other kids, to hang around after school, get in fights." Brandy was still finding work for her son, including roles in the feature films *Sixteen* and *Black Noon* as well as guest appearances on TV shows like *Adam 12*, *Dragnet*, *The Rockford Files*, and *Emergency*. "But my heart was no longer in it," Buddy remembers. "I had also started to smoke marijuana regularly, which further sapped my concentration and focus. Consciously or not, I had made up my mind to quit show business."

Jodie's work had by now become so all-consuming for Brandy that she quit her job and devoted herself full-time to managing her daughter's career. The decision would pay off: Jodie was cast as Audrey in a Warner Bros. film called *Alice Doesn't Live Here Anymore* (1974). Again she played the streetwise child of a way-ward single parent, but this time her character was hardly innocent. She helped lead Tommy, Alice's son, down the path to delinquency by convincing him to get drunk and shoplift with her. And this time the director of the movie was the acclaimed filmmaker Martin Scorsese.

Scorsese was instantly drawn to the waiflike child with a husky voice and a maturity well beyond her years. "In came this little girl with a Lauren Bacall voice," Scorsese later said of Jodie at her audition. He was even more impressed by her talent. "She had total command. A total professional, especially at [her] age . . . is very reassuring. You can rely on their instincts, and their ability to . . . be ready and willing for anything and be in a pretty good mood about it. That's terrific, and it's extremely rare."

Jodie Foster's small role in the Oscar-nominated film marked her transition from playing sweet-faced, wholesome kids to playing wised-up, troublemaking teenagers. It also led to the most controversial role of her career: that of an adolescent prostitute in the 1976 film *Taxi Driver*.

In her most controversial role, 13-year-old Jodie played a young runaway who becomes the focus of an obsessive cab driver. Her role in the dark film Taxi Driver *netted Jodie an Academy Award nomination as Best Supporting Actress.*

4

JUST DOING HER JOB

"I wasn't playing a prostitute in *Taxi Driver*. I was playing a runaway. I don't go for that 'get-into-the-role' stuff," Jodie Foster told an interviewer four years after the movie was released. "I'm a technician, like any other crew member. I do my job and the electrician does his. What I'm good at is making eyes at the camera."

The teenage actress may have viewed her role in the Columbia Pictures film *Taxi Driver* as just another acting job, but many others—including critics, parents, and the city of Los Angeles—did not. The movie tells the gritty story of a New York City cab driver named Travis Bickle (played by Robert DeNiro), an emotionally unstable ex-marine who becomes infatuated with a 12-year-old prostitute named Iris (Foster). Bickle meets Iris when she jumps into his cab one day to escape Sport (Harvey Keitel), the brutal pimp who keeps her on the streets. The cab driver becomes determined to save Iris from prostitution, and the violent way in which he achieves his goal not only adds an ironic twist to the story but also raises the question of whether Travis Bickle is a psychopathic villain or a hero.

Robert DeNiro, who played cabbie Travis Bickle, confers with director Martin Scorsese on the set of Taxi Driver.

The movie's powerful story line and its explicit scenes—including one in which Sport describes the sexual favors Iris can provide, and another in which Bickle and Iris meet in a seedy hotel room—raised a storm of controversy even before the movie was filmed. After word leaked about the movie's adult themes and story line, parents across the country protested that Scorsese and Columbia Pictures were callously exploiting the young actress who had been hired to play Iris. Meanwhile, the welfare board of Los Angeles, having heard about the studio's plan to use a 13-year-old to play a prostitute, stepped in and demanded that Jodie undergo screening by a psychiatrist from the University of California at Los Angeles (UCLA) before she could take the role.

The board's declaration sparked a legal struggle between the California Department of Labor and Brandy Foster, who was outraged at the idea of outsiders determining what was best for her child. "Here was some board trying to tell me what was too adult for my own daughter," she fumed. Determined to win, Brandy enlisted the help of a lawyer, Edmund "Pat" Brown, who would later become the state's governor. However, Brown also recommended that Jodie be interviewed by a mental health specialist. In the end, the UCLA psychiatrist conducted a four-hour interview with Jodie and pronounced her very bright and intuitive—and quite capable of playing the role of Iris without suffering emotional trauma.

Although the Los Angeles welfare board accepted the psychiatrist's assessment, it demanded that one especially revealing scene be cut from the movie and that in explicit scenes Scorsese employ a body double (a person who resembles an actor in build and appearance and stands in during certain scenes). The body double turned out to be Jodie's older sister Connie, then 21; the offending scenes, however, were ultimately cut from the finished movie.

Despite Brandy Foster's willingness to fight for her daughter's right to play Iris, she still seemed surprised at the skill and maturity Jodie displayed in *Taxi Driver*. "I couldn't believe how she looked in her wardrobe," she told *Time* magazine in February 1976. "Suddenly she had legs. I don't think I've ever seen her with her hair curled. I was very happy when she returned to her grubby little self." For her part, Jodie Foster was less than thrilled about the fuss surrounding her role. She dismissed rumors that she had prepared for the role by walking the streets of New York or by working with real-life prostitutes. Nevertheless, Jodie declared, she understood the situations portrayed in the movie. "Listen, kids aren't stupid anymore," she told the *New York Times* in March 1976. "Everybody knows what hookers are. You see them in movies and on TV, you see them on Hollywood Boulevard."

Amid the controversy, Jodie Foster was learning more than simply how to play an unseemly film character. For the first time she was beginning to realize that acting could be a career, not just a way to earn money. And she was discovering that the way to become a truly successful actress was to develop her own technique. In a 1995 interview with *MovieMaker*, Jodie discussed the personal impact of making *Taxi Driver*:

> [Watching movies is] like listening to music if you're a musician. You listen to the parts. When you're aware and attuned to that, you do tend to listen that way, and I've always seen movies that way. . . . At the time of making [*Taxi Driver*] I don't think any of us realized what a classic the film would become and how important it was. But I think we knew we were doing something special. That was a turning point for me because it finally clicked and I realized that [acting] was a real art form and not just something you did after school.

In the end, the only aspect of shooting *Taxi Driver* that Jodie found upsetting was the smell of the fake blood used on the set. And she was right about having worked on "something special": her performance earned her widespread praise, despite the controversy surrounding the movie's release. Critics called her "unusually self-possessed and mature" and said her character had been "superbly played." The recently formed Los Angeles Film Critics Association gave both Foster and Scorsese the first of its New Generation Awards, and at the 1976 Cannes Film Festival in France, *Taxi Driver* received the prestigious Palme d'Or (Golden Palm) award. Most important, her portrayal of Iris netted 13-year-old Jodie Foster an Academy Award nomination for Best Supporting Actress.

Though she didn't win the coveted Oscar, Jodie was pragmatic about the loss: "There are so many grown-up actresses . . . who've never gotten an award; it doesn't

Bugsy Malone, *in which child actors played 1920s-era gangsters and molls, was a departure from the darkness of* Taxi Driver. *The humorous film also starred a young actor named Scott Baio, who would go on to fame on the television series* Happy Days.

seem right to give one to a kid," she said in 1977. Nevertheless, she understood its importance. "If I did get an award, that would mean I could make more money, because the awards are really a way to get your price higher."

Both Jodie Foster's asking price and her fame soared after her Oscar nomination. In the same year that she played Iris, the most sought-after teen actress in Hollywood also landed the main role in a suspense thriller called *The Little Girl Who Lives Down the Lane*. Rynn Jacobs's poet father has died, having made arrangements for Rynn to live secretly on her own—without adult supervision or control—until she turns 18. Rynn needs to fend off a bitter and accusing landlady and the

woman's son, a child molester. Ultimately the girl over-
comes her adversaries "any way she has to"—just as her
father cautioned her to do—and earns her inheritance.

In another 1976 movie, *Bugsy Malone*, Jodie was part
of an all-children cast in a musical takeoff of gangster
movies. The British-made film earned an Academy
Award nomination in America and was named Best
Screenplay by the British Academy; it was also named
Best Film at the Cannes Film Festival. Jodie, who played
a gun moll opposite Scott Baio in the title role, was
hailed by the trade magazine *Variety* as "outstanding."
And the *Washington Post* noted, "[Foster's] precocious-
ness is truly extraordinary, and American filmmakers
ought to guard and nurture it with the proper respect,
because this may be a prodigious talent in the making."

At Cannes, Jodie Foster, now fluent in French, was a
huge hit. Renowned movie critic Roger Ebert recalled
her remarkable poise during the event, which she
attended with Brandy: "[At the press conference,
Jodie] acted as the translator for Scorsese, DeNiro, Keitel . . . [putting] everything into and out of French for
everybody. And I thought to myself, this is an extraordinary person." A film critic for the *Los Angeles Times*
remarked, "She ran the testing course of interviews,
photo calls, and parties with a polite and amused calm
that . . . wowed the journalists."

Jodie may have spoken and behaved like an adult at
the Cannes Film Festival, but she was still struggling
with the uncertainties and heartaches of adolescence.
Her unruffled demeanor when facing the media was
even more impressive given that her beloved Yorkshire
terrier, Napoleon (named after Johnny Whitaker's
screen name in *Napoleon and Samantha*), had died just
before she left for France. "The car arrived to take me
to the Cannes Film Festival," she recounted in a 1995
interview. "[Napoleon] heard the driver at the door
and I think [my dog] was scared—he was yapping and
yapping. He was kind of looking at me and he flew

down the stairs and banged into a wall. And died. He was in convulsions, blood . . . everywhere. I locked myself in the bathroom and wouldn't come out."

For a youngster who coped admirably not only with a demanding academic schedule but also with a full-time, high-profile job, losing her closest companion was devastating. Though her mother offered to get her another pet, Jodie refused even to think of replacing Napoleon. In her adolescent mind the sadness she felt was linked with her newfound fame. After *Taxi Driver* received the Cannes Palme d'Or, Jodie came to the conclusion that "to be successful, I'd had to give up the only thing in my life that I loved and [had to] watch it die in my arms. For the rest of my life [I thought] I would be completely unhappy. . . . For a while [afterward], I didn't want to be successful. . . . I would never mention it. It became a ritual."

"[Jodie] likes to pretend she has no nerves," well-known actress Helen Hayes commented while the two were shooting Candleshoe. *"But when we started the film, I thought I detected that she was a bit tightly strung. So I told her I was nervous, and she confessed that she was nervous, too."*

It would have been understandable for Jodie to take a break from filming to bask in international acclaim and recover from her grief. But she did not slow her pace. The year after she appeared in *Taxi Driver*, *The Little Girl Who Lives Down the Lane*, and *Bugsy Malone*, Jodie fulfilled a contract with Disney Films to star in two of its features, *Freaky Friday* and *Candleshoe*. In the first, Jodie portrays a girl who wishes to change places with her mother and has her wish granted for a day. In *Candleshoe*, which was filmed in Great Britain, Jodie is a hardened Los Angeles street kid named Casey Brown who becomes involved in a scam on a British noblewoman.

Casey is recruited by a con artist named Harry Bundage (Leo McKern) to impersonate the long-lost granddaughter of Lady St. Edmund (played by the distinguished stage actress Helen Hayes). Casey and Bundage travel to Warwickshire, England, where the woman lives in a splendid manor house called Candleshoe. But the woman is not as wealthy as she seems to be: her butler, Priory (David Niven), has been hiding the estate's dire financial situation from his mistress in an attempt to preserve her dignity. Ultimately, Casey develops an affection for the elderly woman and decides not to go through with Bundage's plan.

Jodie Foster seemed unfazed by the prospect of performing with some of the most famous names in acting. In fact, she announced that she preferred to work with adults rather than kids. "I don't feel comfortable working with children," the 14-year-old told *Time* magazine. For all Jodie's bravado, however, her costar Helen Hayes noticed that the teen suffered from jitters just like everyone else on the set. "[Jodie] likes to pretend that she has no nerves," Hayes recalled. "But when we started the film, I thought I detected that she was a bit tightly strung. So I told her I was nervous, and she confessed that she was nervous too."

Although Jodie Foster had earned plenty of work in

Hollywood, *Washington Post* reviewer Gary Arnold's admonition to "guard and nurture" Foster's talent appeared to have been ignored in the years immediately following her Oscar nomination. *Freaky Friday* and *Candleshoe* were box-office disappointments, and another film, *Echoes of a Summer*, in which Jodie plays a terminally ill child, was universally panned by critics. In the summer of 1977 Jodie traveled to Europe with Brandy to shoot two foreign-language films—*Moi, Fleur Bleue* in France (which was released unsuccessfully in the United States as *Stop Calling Me Baby*) and *Il Casotto* in Italy (shown briefly in U.S. theaters as *The Beach House*). At the end of the year Jodie and Brandy returned to Los Angeles. Although Jodie, at 15, continued to attract media attention, she would not appear in another movie until more than two years later, when she was a high school graduate bound for college.

Jodie Foster gives the valedictorian speech at Le Lycée Français de Los Angeles in 1980.

5

A NORMAL LIFE

As the French-speaking valedictorian, Jodie Foster addressed the crowd gathered for the graduation ceremony at Le Lycée Français de Los Angeles in 1980. Having consistently earned straight A's in school, Jodie showed an extraordinary aptitude not only for French language and literature but also for a range of other academic subjects, including philosophy, Italian, Spanish, and world literature.

During her final year at the lycée, Jodie had been busy with exams and college admission applications as well as two film projects, *Carny* and *Foxes*. In *Carny*, Jodie is Donna, a small-town waitress who runs away to join a traveling circus. There she becomes sexually involved with two carnival regulars who are best friends: Frankie, played by Gary Busey, and Patch, played by Robbie Robertson.

Shooting *Carny* was frustrating for the young actress. To one interviewer she confided that she didn't have many lines and therefore spent a great deal of time "improvising in front of the camera" instead. "I prefer it when the lines are given to me, when the responsibility is on someone else," she explained. But Jodie also reveled in the fact that in this movie she didn't have to worry about whether others believed she was mature enough for the role. "The one thing about [playing] Donna is that it's the first time I'm playing a part in which age is not a factor," she said.

Once again, Connie Foster acted as her younger sister's body double in explicit scenes. But Jodie was 17 years old now, and although Brandy Foster was still managing her daughter's film career, Jodie had begun making her own decisions about the roles she would accept. Although relationships between teens and their parents are often trying, Jodie says that when it came to forging her own path, there was very little conflict between her and her mother. Both women claim that it had much to do with the way Jodie was raised. "I think you have to know your child and her moral capacity," Brandy said in 1980. "From the beginning, Jodie was always made to recognize her self-worth. She was encouraged to voice her own opinions on any subject." This openness, Brandy believes, allowed her daughter to confidently take on additional responsibilities once she became a teenager. Jodie agrees, explaining that her mother's role in her life has since changed. "She has a different capacity now in my life," Jodie told *Ladies Home Journal* in 1995. "There was a time when I only wanted her in the professional [capacity] and I didn't want her in the personal, and now it's just the opposite."

Parent-child relationships were the central theme in Jodie's next movie, *Foxes*. The actress played one of four teenage girls growing up in Southern California with little supervision from their dysfunctional parents. Jodie's character, Jeanie, is a world-weary 16-year-old who often finds herself comforting her divorced mother (played by Sally Kellerman). The film marked a milestone for the Fosters—for the first time since Jodie and Buddy were children, they were working together on the same project.

Seven years earlier Buddy Foster had abandoned not only acting but also his family when he left home after a violent argument with Brandy. At first he and two older boys moved into a run-down apartment in Santa Monica. He dropped out of school, took a night job at a fish-and-chips restaurant, and spent his days surfing at the beach. He also began using drugs heavily. For the next few years, Buddy recounts in *Foster Child*, "I drifted through various dead-end jobs, sold pot to friends for spending money, and lived in a tool shed near Venice Beach." Even at his sister Connie's wedding, where he was invited to stand in for his father and give away the bride, Buddy was too intoxicated by drugs to perform the honor.

Only after his mother's friend Aunt Jo gave him a pamphlet about illegal drugs did Buddy begin to realize how badly he was harming himself and the people

In Foxes, *Jodie played a teenager who often had to comfort her divorced mother, played by Sally Kellerman. In this scene from the film, Jodie helps her mother study for an upcoming college exam.*

who cared about him. He made a determined effort to end his substance abuse and took a steady job at a parking concession owned by Connie's husband, Chris Dunn. By the time *Foxes* was in production, Buddy was married and had a three-year-old son named Lucius, and he was eager to return to acting to support his new family. But the lead role he'd hoped to get in the film was given to Scott Baio of the TV series *Happy Days*. Ironically, after Buddy's concerted attempts to get his life back on track, he landed only a minor role in *Foxes*—as a drug-abusing surfer. It was the last acting job he would have.

Despite his own disappointment Buddy was delighted to be working with his sister again. He was impressed not only by the filmmaking experience she had gained over the years, but also by her talent: "It wasn't simply her skill in front of the camera, but the manner in which she interacted with everyone," he wrote. "Jodie never whined, never made excuses, and never asked people to fetch things for her. . . . [She] called everyone from the grips to the truck drivers and cameramen by their first names and would sit and chat with them over lunch."

In 1980, with her film career seemingly back on track, Jodie astounded most of Hollywood by declaring that she was planning to attend college. Among the schools that had accepted her for fall enrollment were such Ivy League universities as Berkeley, Columbia, Harvard, Princeton, Stanford, and Yale. Jodie decided on Yale.

An 18-year-old's announcement that she will be going to college is not usually viewed as a newsworthy event of national proportions. But Jodie Foster's decision was trumpeted in magazines and trade newspapers across the country. *People* magazine, for example, ran a cover story about Jodie, calling her choice "the most startling movie career decision since Garbo chose exile." (Greta Garbo was a renowned Swedish-American actress who retired to a life of seclusion in 1941, at the height

of her film career.) This kind of notoriety was exactly what Jodie had wanted to avoid. One of the advantages of attending college, she believed, was that she could live her life as a normal teenager, away from the constant spotlight of being a film star and with the time and energy to pursue her academic interests. In 1982 she explained what a university education meant to her:

> I wanted to be the kind of girl who's friendly, well-liked, social. To a point, you could say that that's anonymity—the need to be wholly accepted as an equal and yet respected for the product of your efforts. Maybe I was kidding myself. Maybe I was trying to escape from what I felt was an undeserved image. . . . I'd never been to a happy hour, a lacrosse game. . . . [But] I knew everything there was to know about distribution profits and how to handle [film] meetings. . . . Yale was different from any of this.

After much thought, Jodie decided to attend Yale University, the third-oldest institution of higher learning in the United States. Jodie was happy to blend in with the other freshmen attending the school in the fall of 1980.

Here, too, Jodie credited her mother with having reinforced the idea that acting was merely a means to other ends. Brandy, she says, constantly impressed upon her daughter the idea that she could be anything she wanted to be when she grew up. "She tried to give me these other avenues," Jodie told TV interviewer Larry King in 1997. "I just assumed that I'd do something else [other than acting] when I grew up. So, there was no question in my mind that I [would] go to college."

In September 1980 Jodie arrived in New Haven, Connecticut, to begin her freshman year at Yale, registering under her given name, Alicia Christian Foster— a deliberate attempt to separate her movie-star persona from her real life. She signed up for courses in advanced French, freshman English, modern architecture, and diplomatic history. Jodie moved her belongings into Welch Hall on what is called the Old Campus, where she shared a dormitory suite with three other girls.

Jodie was delighted to be able to blend in with the 1,250 other freshmen attending Yale that year. No longer restricted by moviemaking demands, she immersed herself in academic life, setting her own rigorous study schedule and, for the first time, finding companions among her own peers. Adjusting to her new life was difficult at first: even while attending school, Jodie had known only child actors like her and had never had the chance to learn the "rules" of being a regular kid. Now at Yale, she committed herself to fitting in. She traded in her relaxed California attire for preppy tweed jackets and polo shirts. She joined the crew team—but ended up being too small to compete. She hung out with her classmates, binged on junk food, went to football games, stayed up until five in the morning, and attended every freshman event on campus. And after winter break that year she even auditioned for— and won—a part in an off-campus student play called *Getting Out.* By the end of 1980 Jodie declared, "I love Yale totally. I can go any place I want with my friends."

The play marked the first time that Jodie Foster would perform onstage. Despite her years of experience before movie cameras, she had never taken a theater role before. (Her role, ironically, was that of a prostitute who murders a cab driver.) On opening night she warned a reporter who showed up to "talk about the whole play and not just me. . . . Otherwise [the other actors] will kill me."

The play was scheduled to open at the Educational Center for the Arts in New Haven in late March and run until April 5. What happened shortly after the first two performances of *Getting Out*, however, not only stunned the town's residents and the students at Yale, it also shocked the entire nation and resonated around the world.

Jodie Foster went through an intensely difficult time when a fan obsessed with the actress attempted to assassinate the president of the United States to impress her. "Someday I will look back and muse upon the curiosities of history: acting and politics all mixed up together," she wrote in a 1982 Esquire *magazine article. "But for the time being the wounds still ache, the battle goes on."*

6

"WHY ME?"

On the afternoon of March 30, 1981, as President Ronald Reagan left the Washington Hilton Hotel, a man in the crowd drew a .22-caliber gun and fired at the president. One of the bullets struck Reagan and became lodged in his left lung; others hit press secretary James Brady, Secret Service agent Timothy McCarthy, and a local policeman. The president was rushed to a nearby hospital for emergency surgery while the gunman—John W. Hinckley Jr.—was quickly subdued and arrested. Hinckley was taken to a marine base in Quantico, Virginia, and placed in a heavily guarded cell to await questioning and psychiatric evaluation.

Investigators assigned to the case traced the shooter's whereabouts in the days before the assassination attempt and searched each location for clues to his motives. Hinckley had taken a room at the Park Central Hotel, two blocks from the White House. He had also recently stayed in a rooming house in Denver, Colorado. Among his possessions were itineraries for presidential trips, news clippings about the assassination of President John F. Kennedy in 1963, and a letter that had never been mailed. The letter, handwritten by Hinckley, was addressed to Jodie Foster.

"Dear Jodie," it read, "there is a definite possibility that I will be killed in my attempt to get Reagan. . . . As you well know by now I love you very much. Over the past seven months I've left you dozens of poems, letters and love messages in the faint hope that you could develop an interest in me."

From the letter it was clear that Hinckley had visited the campus of Yale and lingered near Jodie's dormitory several times in the previous months. "I would abandon this idea of getting Reagan in a second," he wrote, "if I could only win your heart. . . . The reason I'm going ahead with this attempt now is because I just cannot wait any longer to impress you. I've got to do something now to make you understand, in no uncertain terms, that I am doing all this for your sake!"

In a December 1982 article she wrote for *Esquire* magazine entitled "Why Me?" Jodie Foster described her reaction to the news that she knew the would-be assassin:

> [That] Monday afternoon I was skipping hand in hand across campus with my best friend. Someone yelled as we went by, "Hey. Did you hear? Reagan got shot." . . . At dinnertime everybody was asking if we'd heard what the president's condition was. . . . No one seemed to mention Brady or the assailant until late into the evening. I finally sauntered [back to the dorm] about 10:30. My roommate opened the door before I could get my key in.
> "John," she said.
> "John who?"
> "John Hinckley."
> "What about him? Did he write me again?"
> "He's the one, I think. It was on the radio."

Jodie barely had time to reply before the dean of the university called to tell her that her address and photos "had been found on the arrested man. I felt the tears welling up in my eyes. My body started shaking and I knew that I had lost control," she wrote, "maybe for the very first time in my life."

Three men—secret service agent Timothy J. McCarthy (foreground), Washington, D.C., policeman Thomas K. Delehanty (center), and presidential press secretary James Brady (back)—lie wounded in the wake of John W. Hinckley Jr.'s attack on President Ronald Reagan March 30, 1981. Reagan, who was also wounded, was rushed to the hospital in a waiting limousine.

The dean told her that FBI representatives were with him and wanted to speak with her immediately. But Jodie didn't go directly to the dean's office. First she ran to the dorm room of a good friend. While she waited for the friend to come out of the shower, she tried to joke with a few students down the hall about the news, "to prove to myself I could do it," she later said. Once she was alone with her friend, however, she burst into tears. And then she began to laugh—but it was hardly joyous laughter. "[It] was strange and hollow, and I couldn't control it. It was beyond me. My body jerked in painful convulsions. I hurt."

Even more upsetting for Foster was that investiga-

John Hinckley Jr. is transferred from a federal prison in North Carolina, where he had been undergoing psychological tests, to the U.S. Marine base at Quantico, Virginia. Investigators searching Hinckley's belongings after the shooting found an unmailed letter to Jodie Foster, in which he discussed his plan to shoot the president in order to get her attention.

tors of Hinckley's assassination attempt learned that he developed his obsession with her after seeing her in *Taxi Driver*. As a result, nearly every media account of the story was accompanied by a photo of 13-year-old Jodie dressed as Iris. Moreover, information "was being leaked so fast," Jodie wrote, "that the news stations knew more than any of us on the inside. I had to read a local newspaper to learn most of the details."

Two days later, after lengthy interviews with the Secret Service and the FBI, and after consulting with Yale officials, local district attorneys, and policemen, the student-actress called a press conference. In a lounge at Calhoun College, Jodie met with six invited reporters and explained how she came to know about Hinckley. Beginning in late 1980, she said, she had begun receiving "unsolicited correspondence" from the love-struck man. She emphasized that none of the letters she received had mentioned Hinckley's plan to assassinate the president. In fact, she stated, he had made no threats to harm anyone, including her. To queries about the violence in *Taxi Driver* inspiring Hinckley, she said: "I really am not here to answer questions about [that]. . . . As far as I was concerned, there was no message [of violence] from [it]. It was a piece of fiction. . . . It's not meant to inspire people to do anything."

As she answered the reporters' questions, Jodie seemed poised and calm, just as they had come to expect from the self-assured actress. Inside, however, Jodie was shocked and confused. She was also beginning to understand the harsh realities of being a celebrity. "I knew that these were the faces, the uncomfortable, fascinated eyes, that I would have to meet for the rest of my life," she wrote in *Esquire*. "If they wanted weakness, I wasn't about to give it to them."

The worst part of the ordeal came after the reporters had gone home and some of the excitement had died down. "Everyone had been kind, sympathetic, availing," Jodie remembered. "My mother would take my hand and say, 'Don't worry.' The administration [of Yale] assured me . . . that they were available at a moment's notice. Even the reporters I'd come to know would pat me on the back and say, 'Hang in there, kid.' But their offerings only stressed the fact that I was completely alone." Jodie began to feel as though she had split into two people—the confident actress that people saw on the movie screen, and a second Jodie, who was "shrouded in bravado and wit and was, underneath, a creature crippled, without self-esteem, a frail and alienated being."

Less than a week after Hinckley's assassination attempt, *Getting Out* was scheduled for a second and final weekend of performances at New Haven's Educational Center for the Arts. Most people assumed that Foster would not appear, given the recent media attention and the obvious concern for her safety. She did perform, however, although she later regretted the disruption her presence caused. "It was something I had to do, some damn foolish thing I had to prove to myself. No one could just change my life, my plans, without asking me. No one could keep me down. . . . As long as everyone was going to stare, I might as well play the game full out," Jodie wrote.

During the first performance Jodie was startled to hear the sound of a motorized camera coming from the audience. In the heightened security surrounding the event, audience members had been forbidden to bring cameras and were being frisked at the entrance to the theater. She peered past the stage lights toward the sound and saw a bearded man sitting quietly with a fixed stare that she found unnerving. She heard the noise again during the second night's performance and saw the man in the same seat, although she could not tell whether he was the source of the sound. On the third night both the sound and the bearded man were gone—but during intermission a chilling note was posted on the lobby bulletin board. "By the time the show is over," it read, "Jodie Foster will be dead."

Jodie was just beginning to recover from the experience when, a few days later, an anonymous and threatening letter was slipped under her dorm-room door (she had been assigned a single room after the Hinckley incident). She immediately gave the letter to officials, who assigned her round-the-clock bodyguards. The next morning, after her English class, a guard informed her that Secret Service agents and the local police had apprehended the letter writer. He was a 22-year-old bearded man from Pennsylvania named Edward M. Richardson, who had been arrested in New York while traveling by bus from New Haven to Washington, D.C. He was carrying a loaded .32-caliber gun, with which he apparently intended to shoot the president. Upon his arrest Richardson revealed that he had originally targeted Jodie herself, but that he had seen her perform in *Getting Out* and decided that she was too pretty to kill.

Jodie Foster was thrown into an emotional tailspin from which she would not emerge for months. Learning about the proximity of the second would-be assassin "felt like a ton of steel dropping from the top of a 30-story building," she wrote in *Esquire*. She continued:

> Death. So simple, so elementary, so near. Pulling a trigger is as easy as changing the TV channel with remote control. What was I trying to prove by performing a college play three days after one of the most bizarre assassination attempts of our time? Who was I trying to impress? Why was it so important to look death in the eye and hurl victorious insults? . . .

> I started perceiving death in the most mundane but dis-
> tressing events. Being photographed felt like being shot; it
> still does. I thought everyone was looking at me in
> crowds; perhaps they were. . . . People were punishing me
> because I was there. They were sending bullets, pulling
> triggers, exercising the simple law of cause and effect. . . .
>
> I could feel death by alienating and insulting the peo-
> ple I loved or at least enjoyed. I could feel it by hating
> myself so much that I hated everyone around me for lik-
> ing me. I died when I looked at myself in the mirror, the
> body that no longer slept, the clothes I no longer cared for,
> the mismatched socks, the tired expression, the reddened
> eyes. . . . I became suspicious of everyone.

The Hinckley ordeal, Jodie Foster declared, "did not
destroy my anonymity; it only destroyed the illusion of
it. Every man or woman in this world had the right to
stare at, point at, and judge me because . . . [as an
actress] that was my job. That's what I got paid for—to
take my lumps."

In May 1981, after her freshman year ended, a
greatly changed Jodie Foster returned to Los Angeles,
where she spent the first two weeks of summer break
at a health spa in the California mountains. She tried
to reconcile the events of the previous months with
her own goals. It seemed obvious to Jodie that the
Hinckley and Richardson incidents were a direct result
of her being a celebrity. Her fame had intruded on the
carefully constructed "normal" life she had sought—
and found—as a college student at Yale. And though
family, friends, and fans were sympathetic, she believed
that they all felt pity and embarrassment for her. "And
if this was show business," she reasoned, "I wanted no
part of it. I didn't belong there."

Although Jodie worked on a film that summer—a
movie called *O'Hara's Wife*, for which she had signed a
contract the previous year—she couldn't shake the feeling of being a target, someone so recognizable that she
could easily become the victim of another disturbed

assassin. Despite the fact that Hinckley and Richardson had contacted her at college, she saw Yale as a safe haven and longed to return there in the fall, escaping the "untrustworthy" atmosphere of Los Angeles.

By the time she did go back in September 1981, everything seemed to have returned to normal on campus. Her spirits improved; she began to dress better, eat more healthful foods, keep her room tidier, and return phone calls. Before long, however, she found that her usually intense interest in schoolwork was beginning to wane. "I found myself watching movies every night," she wrote in *Esquire.* "I was getting restless. 'Just school' wasn't enough."

Like most successful actors, Jodie regularly received screenplays in the mail from directors, screenwriters, and producers eager to cast her in their next film. Soon after she began her sophomore year at Yale, a script arrived that caught her attention. Titled *Svengali,* the film was based on the 1931 classic starring the leg-

Jodie returned to the screen in Svengali, *a 1983 television movie that also starred Peter O'Toole. Although* Svengali *was a flop, she felt that it healed the pain of the Hinckley incident and rekindled her desire to act.*

endary film actor John Barrymore. This version would feature Peter O'Toole as a has-been music star who mentors a young pop singer in search of stardom (the part offered to Jodie). Even more appealing, the movie was to be filmed on location in New York City, not far from New Haven. "I was ecstatic," Jodie remembers. "For the first time in two years, I fell in love with a [film] project."

Jodie eagerly signed on, and though *Svengali* was a critical failure, she found that her old enthusiasm for her craft had come back. The project "made me fall in love with acting again. It cured me of most of the insecurities; it healed my wounds." By the time she was summoned to Washington, D.C., in the spring of 1982 to give a deposition for the trial of John Hinckley Jr., she felt self-assured and calm—even though no one had told her that Hinckley himself would be present at the procedure. "I played cowboy and got through it the best way I knew how," she later recalled.

That night, as she watched the Academy Award presentations on the TV in her hotel room, she realized that pretending to be brave when one feels insecure or scared is part of human nature. "I thought about how [just] dealing with another human being was an unconscious act of bravado," she wrote in *Esquire*. "I decided that night that good actors are essentially good liars. . . . When we 'turn on' to the camera . . . we aren't only manipulating a lens and some glass fragments. We're talking to 10, 20, or perhaps 30 million people." Thus it wasn't hard to imagine why Hinckley would see her on the movie screen and believe that he knew her, she reasoned. That was part of her art. What made his behavior criminal was that he confused love with obsession and used violence as a way to communicate.

But she had survived the ordeal, both physically and emotionally, and that was what mattered most. "The truth [is] that in the crunch, when the chips are down, in a time of crisis, you resort to strength you'd never dreamed you owned. . . . The will to survive," Jodie Foster concluded, "is stronger than any emotion."

A haunted-looking Jodie as Sarah Tobias in The Accused.

7

THE PERFECT ACTING MACHINE

The remainder of Jodie Foster's college career passed with little fanfare, although daily reminders of the Hinckley and Richardson incidents remained in the form of constant security guards and extra safety precautions. While Jodie continued to work toward her bachelor's degree, she also eagerly returned to acting, making movies during school vacations and occasional semester-long sabbaticals.

Her next feature film, *The Hotel New Hampshire*, began shooting in early 1983 in Quebec, Canada. Based on John Irving's novel of the same name, the movie is about the eccentric Berry family headed by Win, the owner of the hotel in which they live. As Franny, the high-spirited oldest daughter who, ironically, ends up becoming a movie star, Jodie Foster was joined by a youthful cast that included Beau Bridges, Nastassja Kinski, Amanda Plummer, Matthew Modine, and Rob Lowe.

From the start Jodie reveled in the convivial atmosphere of the *Hotel New Hampshire* set. Even the older actors, such as Wallace Shawn and Wilford Brimley, seemed to relish the camaraderie of the younger cast members. "Everyone in [the movie] was under 25, and even those who weren't were," Jodie quipped. She felt a special kinship to actress Nastassja Kinski, who played Susie the Bear, an Ivy League–college dropout who sports a tattered bear costume when she goes out in public. On the set Jodie felt safe for the first time in years. *The Hotel New Hampshire* received mixed reviews from the critics, but once again Jodie Foster defended her work. "I think it's wonderful," she said of the picture. "No matter what flaws are in there, it has a heart that I've never seen ever again."

For her next film Jodie returned to one of her best-loved retreats—Paris, France. In *Le Sang des Autres* (*The Blood of Others*), a TV romance that opens in 1938 at the outbreak of World War II, Foster plays Helene, a French dress designer torn between her boyfriend Jean, a Resistance fighter, and a wealthy German business-man. The movie was panned in America. Jodie main-tained that part of the reason it failed was that the French producers had forbidden her to use a foreign accent for the American cable version of the film, despite her fluency in French. "World War II didn't happen in Ohio," she explained in an August 1984 *TV Guide* interview. "I think [the producers] are underes-timating the audience, but it's out of my control."

And control—not only over her own life but also over the films she made and how they were made—was what Jodie Foster had wanted for years. Since she was a teenager she had declared frequently that she wanted to direct her own films. Her experience with *The Blood of Others* made her even more determined to do so.

Later that year Jodie traveled to New Zealand to film *Mesmerized* (also released as *Shocked*), based on a 19th-century murder that occurred in that country. To most viewers and critics *Mesmerized* was unremarkable. But sharp-eyed readers of the credits might have noticed that in addition to playing a lead role, Jodie Foster was listed as a coproducer. After 18 years of acting, she had finally managed to get beyond the camera lens and

behind the scenes on a movie set.

In May 1985—a year after her classmates—Jodie Foster received her bachelor's degree in African-American literature from Yale University. Earning an academic degree is a great accomplishment for any student, and Jodie was proud of her achievement. "College demanded 100 percent and my movie career demanded 100 percent, so it was very tough to do both and do them well," she told an interviewer in 1987. Although Jodie had talked about getting a graduate degree, becoming a novelist, or perhaps seeking a position as U.S. ambassador, by the time she graduated she had one goal: to remain in the film industry. Recalling her childhood, when her mother encouraged her and Buddy to use acting as a means to achieve other goals, Jodie

Jodie with Hotel New Hampshire *costar Nastassja Kinski. The actress later admitted that she loved the closeness of the cast while the film was being made: "I felt we were really family. . . . When we finished the picture, we were all teary-eyed . . . and we knew we would never be like this again."*

A reflective moment for Jodie Foster during the film Stealing Home.

explained, "I always thought actors were stupid, and I thought if I went to college I wouldn't be a stupid actor. But I realized what I really wanted to do was to act and there was nothing stupid about it at all. It's like going to another country—you learn about chopsticks and all that, but what you really learn is about yourself."

But the next few movies Jodie Foster made were so poorly received that although she earned consistently favorable reviews, some critics began to wonder whether the 25-year-old actress's best film years were behind her. The *Los Angeles Daily News* called the 1987 psychological thriller *Siesta* "an extremely strong contender for the most irritating movie of the year. It mushes all the most grating qualities of the European 'art' film into one unendurable hash." Foster at least received some praise. "*Siesta* has scarcely more depth than a student film, but Foster larks out on an acting class exercise and erases everyone in range from the screen," wrote J. Hoberman in the *Village Voice*. "The real question [is,] when is someone going to come up with a movie to match Foster's potential?"

Jodie Foster's next film, *Five Corners* (1988), fared no better with film critics, but her convincing performance earned her the Independent Spirit Award for Best Actress in 1989. Set in 1964, the dramatic comedy follows the lives of several inhabitants of a Bronx, New York, neighborhood known as Five Corners. In a chilling echo of real life, Foster, who shared top billing with John Turturro and Tim Robbins, played Linda, a quiet and prim girl who is targeted by a disturbed neighborhood boy (Turturro). In *Stealing Home*, which was released the same year, Foster played Katie Chandler, a free-spirited, well-off suburban girl who baby-sits 10-year-old Bill Wyatt and then ends up years later as his first serious girlfriend. The movie relied on flashbacks that unfold when Billy (Mark Harmon) returns home after Katie's suicide.

Stealing Home garnered a bit more praise from the critics than Jodie's previous films had—one described Foster as bringing "breezy pizzazz" to the movie—and it even earned an enthusiastic following. For the actress herself, however, the most valuable aspect of working on the film was the opportunity to collaborate with the directors. By this time she was actively searching for a project that she could direct, and she was reading nearly every script she could get her hands on. Always fascinated with the behind-the-scenes aspects of producing a movie, the veteran actress had learned a great deal about the jobs of film crew members and their equipment. In fact, unlike most film celebrities, Jodie considered herself a "blue-collar worker" just like the crews with whom she worked. In his 1995 book *Jodie: A Biography*, author Louis Chunovic describes Foster's penchant for learning about the nuts and bolts of moviemaking:

> [She] was genuinely interested—she knew about lights and filters and camera lenses and focal lengths—and that fascination enchanted her coworkers. She even knew film crews, telling one interviewer that the "best crew is a New York crew on location outside of New York City." . . .
>
> Foster was known for the long hours she liked to spend on the set, time when she could have been elsewhere. Most movie stars couldn't wait to play hooky, typically rushing away from their scenes on location to their lavishly appointed Winnebago trailers.

One of the best scripts Foster came across was titled *Witness*, a story of a young waitress who is gang-raped in a local bar and ends up with a high-powered female deputy district attorney to prosecute her attackers and the onlookers. The screenplay was so powerful, she recalled years later, that "I did everything I could to get it." The film's director, Jonathan Kaplan, made a case for hiring Jodie to play the main character, but producers Stanley Jaffe and Sherry Lansing seemed hesitant. Finally they asked for a meeting with the actress.

Jodie Foster harbored no illusions about why they wanted to meet with her. Her most recent films had been disappointments; moreover, she knew that they wanted to see whether she had slimmed down since her college days, during which she had gained about 20 pounds. "Well," she told Kaplan after the meeting, "I met with Stanley Jaffe, and he saw I'm no longer fat."

Foster had known since childhood that in Hollywood appearances are everything, but she had learned not to take it to heart. "At some point, you've got to accept that you're an object," she told *Rolling Stone* magazine in 1991. "It's not personal, but ultimately somebody's going to say your voice sucks and your body sucks, too. You have to learn to make the personal not so personal." That practical acceptance of film-star reality was part of the reason Jodie Foster became the producers' first choice to play Sarah Tobias. After watching Foster's screen test, Sherry Lansing was awestruck. "She just said, 'The envelope please,'" Kaplan recalled, referring to the sealed envelopes in which Oscar winners' names are placed before they are announced.

Jodie Foster immersed herself in the movie with great fervor. Hired to play district attorney Katheryn Murphy was popular actress Kelly McGillis, who had starred in a 1985 thriller that was also titled *Witness,* as well as the 1986 hit *Top Gun.* (During shooting, the title of Foster's movie was changed to *Reckless Endangerment* to avoid confusion with the 1985 film; it was later changed again, to *The Accused,* before it was released in theaters.) On the emotionally charged set Foster and McGillis—a classically trained actress— quickly became close friends, and Jodie learned a great deal from her costar's approach to acting. "I say things off the top of my head, but when Kelly says something it's usually dead-on," Foster said. "She's also deeply emotional. . . . She's very real and she doesn't lie. . . . She doesn't know how to."

Ironically, Foster's role is that of a physically and psychologically abused—and justifiably angry—young woman who struggles to come to terms with her rape, while McGillis plays a cool, almost emotionless lawyer who strives to remain detached from her working-class client but cannot distance herself from what happened to her. For this reason, Foster believes that the core of the movie is not the rape and its aftermath but the way in which Sarah Tobias and Katheryn Murphy learn from each other. "It's about how they change each other's prejudices and problems," Foster explained. "Each of them is cut off from something the other possesses, and by . . . having someone care they become whole."

As she had with the cast and crew of *The Hotel New Hampshire,* Foster also developed close bonds with her coworkers on the set of *The Accused,* which eased the strain of performing the most gut-wrenching scenes. And for the first time since she was a teenager, Jodie enlisted her mother, Brandy, to be on the set during filming. "I've come to realize I need [a family member] for the first couple of weeks [of taping], because I not only get lonely but disoriented," Jodie said later that year. "She's a friend, more and more so. She's always been my friend."

That sentiment was echoed in Jodie Foster's acceptance speech at the Academy Awards ceremony the following spring, during which the 26-year-old actress received her first Oscar for her performance in *The Accused* and thanked her "tribes"—and especially her mother—for providing support and strength. But her success was also a result of years of hard work and her determination to portray realistic, down-to-earth women who set out to prove that they are better than others believe they are. Some years later, Jon Amiel, the director of the 1993 film *Sommersby*, described the supreme professionalism with which Jodie Foster practices her craft:

> She can be sitting, joking in French to the makeup man, with chewing gum and her glasses on. You say, "Jodie, you're on," and within 30 seconds she's in front of the camera, delivering a scene that will break your heart. . . . Jodie combines all the technical facility of a child actor with the maturity of a really seasoned campaigner. If God had designed a perfect acting machine, it would be pretty close to Jodie.

Foster's next movie, *Backtrack*, starring Dennis Hopper as a hit man obsessed with Jodie's artist character, was not what most people expected from an Oscar-winning actress. (The film never appeared in American movie theaters because the distributor, Vestron, went bankrupt before its release.) But Jodie had already moved on—to directing films—and this was not what most people expected from her either.

Why change courses now, her advisers asked her, when she appeared to be on the fast track to another Oscar? "Nobody wanted me to direct a movie right after I won an Academy Award—it was like, 'Come on, go out, get some performances, this is your big chance.' And it all made sense, but sometimes you have to do things that make sense for *you*," Foster said in an interview about her debut as a director for the film *Little Man Tate*.

Although she had never put much stock in acting awards, she now realized that receiving one had suddenly opened doors for her. "Projects that could not get done [before] now get done because you say you want to do it," she said with wonder a few months after receiving the Oscar. And if an Academy Award was what she needed to pursue her passion for directing, then Jodie Foster was more than happy to put the golden statuette to good use.

As The Accused *was filmed, Jodie and costar Kelly McGillis (left) became close friends. "She has really taught me things," Foster said of McGillis afterward. "Some had to do with her training, but most came from the way she thinks and feels."*

A dramatic scene from The Silence of the Lambs. *Jodie received great praise—and numerous awards—for her role as FBI agent Clarice Starling in the psychological thriller.*

8

AN EVERYDAY HERO

The script for *Little Man Tate* had been making the rounds in Hollywood for years before Jodie Foster read it. She was instantly attracted to the story of Dede Tate, a single parent with a blue-collar job and a seven-year-old whiz-kid son named Fred. The boy genius longs for normalcy while he balances his mother's checkbook and disassembles her phone to see how it works. Fred comes to the attention of Dr. Jane Grierson, who runs an institute for gifted children, and Dede's emotional tug-of-war—whether to keep her son at home or risk losing him by sending him to the institute where his potential can be developed—is at the heart of the tale.

The obvious draw for Jodie Foster was the idea of making a movie about a single-parent family, but she was also taken with the overall theme of being a misfit. "They're all misfits," she said of the three main characters. "Dede because she refuses to be conventional . . . [Dr. Grierson] because she is tragically bereft [of emotions]. . . . In trying to create a world where he fits in, [Fred] creates a world for the misfits around him. [The movie] is not a quest for conventional happiness."

Jodie took on the challenge of directing and acting in Little Man Tate, *a film about a woman with a genius son. Here, she discusses a scene with nine-year-old costar Adam Hann-Byrd.*

Scott Rudin, then the production director at Twentieth Century Fox, had no qualms about hiring Foster to direct—and star in—*Little Man Tate*. "She's technically proficient beyond belief—very skilled in the process of what it means to make a film," he said in a 1991 interview. "And she's got a lot of stamina. Very stalwart—there's nothing that can happen on a set that she hasn't seen."

The most difficult aspect of the project for Foster, it turned out, was acting, not directing. Dede Tate, the actress said, was extremely difficult to capture because the role required her to express emotions she had never shown on-screen. Where nearly all of Foster's previous roles had been strong-willed, determined characters, she now needed to show a woman with a big heart and a great capacity for love. Another reason the job was difficult was that, unlike directing, Jodie found acting mentally exhausting. "It's tiring to have your whole job be about pleasing someone else—pleasing the lighting guy, pleasing the audience. And then also maintaining the [personality] of the character," she explained. As the director, on the other hand, she called the shots. "When you're in control of everything . . . you just make the decision and move on," she said some years later in a *Larry King Live* interview. "It's a wonderful feeling . . . to know that . . . the entire vision of the film is in your hands, that every decision is yours." Not surprisingly, the cast and crew of *Little Man Tate* agreed that Jodie Foster the director was a consummate professional. Sporting a jacket with the initials BLT (for "Bossy Little Thing," a nickname given to her by Jonathan Kaplan, the director of *The Accused*), Foster navigated her set with confidence and good sense. She believed that she had a responsibility to the people who worked for her to be prepared for everything. "Films are too important not to have a drawn road map. . . . When I come into a shot, I always have an idea," she says. But she was also known to be motherly and affectionate with her workers, occasionally cooking a weekend breakfast for the entire cast and crew or holding an employee's child on her lap while directing a scene.

The first-time director was especially patient with her nine-year-old costar, Adam Hann-Byrd, who played the title role. When Adam first appeared on the set, Jodie greeted him with a series of playacting karate chops, which he gleefully returned. After spending some time with the boy, Foster began to see that Adam was a very "realistic kid," so she decided to "load him up with a lot of technical things—kids usually connect with the technical—and then he would just relax," Foster explains. "Or I'd say, 'Make your eyebrows like you're scared,' and that would make him a little nervous. And then I'd get what I wanted." What she also wanted, she said, was to create an atmosphere in which the young actor would feel so comfortable that he would want to return to acting again and again, just as she had done herself.

Did Jodie Foster see parallels between the characters in *Little Man Tate* and her own childhood? Of course, she admitted, but she stressed that she was not trying to make an autobiographical film. Still, she does believe that the "sensitive and analytical" aspects of Fred Tate's character match her own childhood personality. In addition, Foster knows from experience that the bond between a single mother and her child differs from that of a child with two parents, because the single mother needs to play many more roles in that child's life. "There's a certain kind of romance that a single parent has with [her] child. . . . A kind of authoritarian thing, and a kind of vulnerability that you don't have when there are two parents," she says. "It is a very peculiar phenomenon, and I can't say that [it] doesn't affect my dealing with Fred and Dede."

Audiences, critics, and even fellow directors greeted the fall 1991 premiere of *Little Man Tate* with enthusiasm. Calling Foster simply "wonderful" in the role of Dede Tate, the *Hollywood Reporter* crowed, "First-time director Jodie Foster has presented a stirring and magnificent portrait of the human spirit . . . with a supremely sensitive eye toward the boy's terrifying limbo-like childhood." One of Jodie Foster's favorite directors, French filmmaker Louis Malle, declared, "Jodie's film is basically about the profound loneliness of childhood, and she's dealt with it head-on. I would be very happy and proud to have made the film that she did."

Especially praised was Foster's ability to keep her immediate objectives of acting and directing in line with a larger goal. A *Washington Post* reporter wrote, "No actress working today has orchestrated a career that shows the same immaculate sense of forethought, design, and consistency of purpose that Foster's does. Nor does the work of any other actress resonate so heavily with her own life. Like Foster herself, almost all of [her] characters are from working-class backgrounds; most are extraordinarily precocious and knowledgeable about the world of adults—even the secret parts of grown-up life."

What many fans didn't know, however, was that the film was almost tabled before it was released. Shortly before Foster began working on *Little Man Tate*, she had finished shooting another film, *The Silence of the Lambs*. Based on the best-selling thriller by Thomas Harris, the movie, not yet released, would feature Foster as an ambitious rookie FBI agent named Clarice Starling, whose first assignment is to track down a serial killer. Her costar was Anthony Hopkins, who played another serial killer, an imprisoned madman nicknamed "Hannibal the Cannibal" whose help Starling desperately needs to catch the murderer.

Both films were produced by Orion Pictures, which Foster chose because of their hands-off policy toward directors. That year she had announced a two-year, first-look agreement with the studio to star in, direct, and produce films. ("First-look" means that Foster was obligated to offer Orion the right to bid first on any of her projects.) But during the editing of *Little Man Tate*, Orion Pictures ran into financial trouble and was forced to decide between releasing Foster's movie or another big-name film, *Blue Sky*. As a result, Jodie found herself fighting with Orion executives for the funds needed to release and promote her film. Although *Little Man Tate* made it into the theaters, just two months after its premiere Orion declared bankruptcy.

"In the course of doing that I started acting like a producer," Foster said with pride, "and I realized I liked that." She set about forming her own production company, which she called Egg Pictures. After a year of negotiating with PolyGram Filmed Entertainment (PFE), which was not a studio but a production and distribution network, Jodie Foster sealed a deal that was unprecedented in Hollywood.

While many high-powered actors work out arrangements with studios to film their own projects, the studio itself normally retains the right to approve most creative decisions. But Foster's agreement with PFE in effect made her into her own studio: she had the final say not only on which movies she wanted to make, but also on whom she would cast and whether she would act in them, direct them, or produce them. She also retained the right to decide who would distribute each movie. PFE agreed to fund up to six films in three years and to provide from $10 million to $25 million per picture.

"The irony is that Jodie could do whatever she wants to do without a company [of her own]," says Scott Frank, the screenwriter of *Little Man Tate* and a friend of Jodie's. "She doesn't need the housekeeping details of Egg. In Hollywood . . . starting your own company can seem like freedom. But the deal you make . . . is that then you have to work for yourself!" And that's just what Jodie Foster wanted to do. "[The agreement gives me] more control over my destiny," she told a trade journal in 1992. "I want signature films. . . . I've always been driven by material, not price."

Jodie Foster's name and reputation were about to assume even more weight with the release of *The Silence of the Lambs*. Director Jonathan Demme had initially offered the part of FBI agent Clarice Starling to Michelle Pfeiffer. But Pfeiffer could not reconcile herself with the "darkness" of the role—which was precisely what drew Foster to the character. "I love getting to that place of seeing things that people don't ever get to see. . . . That's what fuels me," she said during filming.

The combination of Jodie Foster and Anthony Hopkins, who had a similar reputation as a precise and

Critics called Little Man Tate *a "moving, extraordinarily empathic look at a child genius. . . . Beautifully realized by Foster in her directing debut; her [acting] performance is equally strong."*

intellectual actor, turned out to be electric. Foster was surprised several times during shooting when Hopkins elicited reactions from her by performing unexpectedly. For example, in one key scene, in which Starling first meets Lecter face-to-face through the bars of his high-security "cage," Hopkins began to mimic the backwoods accent that Foster adopted for her character. Foster was stunned by the unscripted performance. "Tears came to my eyes. It was so hurtful. As an actress, I was thinking, 'This guy's making fun of my accent!' It was a moment when the boundary got very fuzzy between me and Clarice," she told one interviewer. But she also realized that "it was the perfect thing for Lecter to do, because Clarice has been hiding her rural accent, trying to . . . escape her origins in a certain way. And here's a guy who nails her."

Hopkins was equally impressed with his costar's performance. Referring to another scene in which his character hisses at Starling and Foster barely flinches, he said, "She works with such economy. She doesn't do a thing, and yet you can see all the thoughts going through her eyes, like 'Oh my God, this man is an animal, a beast.' And I think that's the great skill of an actress like Jodie—it just shows on her face; she doesn't have to *act* it."

To prepare for her role, Foster spent a week with trainees at the FBI Academy in Quantico, Virginia, attending courses and seminars and keeping up with their required fitness regimen. She wasn't the only person who was determined to create a true-to-life film; Demme also consulted John E. Douglas, the head of the FBI's Investigative Support Services Unit, to add authenticity to the project. Both actress and director believed that the movie—far from being a run-of-the-mill Hollywood "slasher"—conveyed an important message. "Serial killers exist," Demme said plainly. "We live in a society that permits [this kind of abuse], to an appalling extent. . . . We want to be harrowing—and really, just as appalling and frightening as this whole subject is."

When *The Silence of the Lambs* premiered in February 1991, both the film and its stars earned high praise. "Foster, with amazing delicacy, shows us the constant tension between the character's emotions and her actions," said *New Yorker* magazine. The *New York Daily News* found her "totally riveting." *Glamour* magazine later named Foster "Woman of the Year," declaring that "her bright Clarice Starling was the first

The biggest film of 1991–92, The Silence of the Lambs *swept the Academy Awards, winning for Best Picture, Best Actor (Anthony Hopkins), Best Actress (Jodie, shown here with Hopkins), and Best Screenplay.*

woman detective in memory who didn't appear in her underwear, spring [around] in high heels, or fall in love with a killer." Audiences apparently agreed: by the end of the year *The Silence of the Lambs* had become the third-highest-grossing movie of 1991. By the time the Oscars were announced the following spring, it had earned $245 million worldwide.

Silence was not without detractors, however. Early in its publicity campaign, gay advocacy groups began protesting the film's depiction of the serial murderer at large as a cross-dressing, effeminate man. They argued that the movie portrayed homosexuals in the worst possible light, as predatory killers. One publication, *Out-week*, known for its controversial practice of "outing" (revealing the sexual orientation of celebrities presumed to be gay without their consent, and often despite evidence to the contrary), threatened to out Foster herself in retaliation for her appearance in the movie. The action earned her a sympathetic following among others, gay and straight, who believed that the magazine had violated her privacy. Nevertheless, the debates continued up to, and even following, the Academy Awards ceremony in the spring of 1992.

The Silence of the Lambs and its cast and crew were showered with honors, including seven Academy Award nominations and five Oscars: Best Picture, Best Actor (Hopkins), Best Adapted Screenplay and Best Director (Demme), and Best Actress for Jodie Foster—her second Academy Award. Foster and Hopkins also won the British Best Actress and Actor awards, respectively, and Foster earned a Golden Globe Best Actress award.

In her Oscar acceptance speech Jodie Foster once again thanked friends and family for their strength and devotion. But she also paid tribute to another "tribe," to reuse a term she had used three years earlier:

> I'd like to dedicate this award to all the women who came before, who never had the chances I've had, and the survivors, and the pioneers, and the outcasts . . . and to all the people in this industry who have respected my choices and not been afraid of the power and dignity that entitled me to. . . .Thanks to the academy for embracing such an incredibly strong and beautiful feminist hero that I'm so proud of.

After the success of *Little Man Tate* and *The Silence of the Lambs*, Jodie Foster again chose to break new ground by taking on her first romantic role. *Sommersby*, loosely based on the 1983 French film *The Return of Martin Guerre*, is the story of Jack Sommersby (Richard Gere), a Civil War veteran who returns after years of battle to his wife, Laurel (Foster). Mrs. Sommersby doubts that the gentleman she has now come to love is the same cruel, drunken man she was married to before the war. The neighbors are also suspicious. Is the man really Jack Sommersby or a clever impostor? In the climactic ending the man who calls himself Sommersby can save himself only by renouncing the identity he has claimed.

Many Hollywood insiders believed that *Sommersby* would never measure up to its Academy Award–nominated predecessor. Moreover, Jodie Foster was not a conventional leading lady. "A lot of people questioned [the casting]," producer Steven Reuther told an interviewer in 1993. "And it was a gamble, because there are the obvious romantic leading females, and Jodie really is not one of them. Also, I don't think anyone had ever seen Jodie in a period costume. But once we got her in the [19th-century] clothes [we asked ourselves], 'How could there have been a question?'"

Foster herself, as usual referring to acting as simply a "skill," agreed with Reuther. "You look at some tintypes [a kind of 19th-century photograph], you wear a hoop skirt for a week, and it will come to you," she said. "Not that it's so easy. There is nothing worse than an actor who puts on a pair of breeches and speaks in the same bad California accent that he walked in with. But for me it's all a game," Foster said. "You use everything: a painting that you saw, something somebody said. Anything that works."

Although Laurel Sommersby was a new type of role for Jodie Foster, she believed that the character was at heart the same kind of person she had been playing since childhood: an unconventional woman doing her best to remain strong and rise above social conventions.

While still searching for her first producing project for Egg Pictures, Foster took on another unconventional character. This time, however, she decided to become a comedian. Based on a popular ABC television series of the late 1950s and early 1960s, *Maverick* costars Mel Gibson in the title role and features James Garner, the original Maverick, as Marshal Zane Cooper.

Jodie turned to physical comedy in Maverick, *a film based on the popular television show of the late 1950s and early 1960s. Mel Gibson (left) had the title role as Bret Maverick, while James Garner (right), who had played the original Maverick in the television series, had a part as a lawman.*

More than one critic noted that the cast, including the usually serious Foster, seemed to be having a great time in front of the cameras. But Jodie had not been the first choice: both Gibson and director Richard Donner had originally approached Meg Ryan, who turned the project down to spend time with her new baby. After Foster's first reading, however, they were convinced that she was perfect for the part.

Despite what some of her associates thought, Jodie had chosen the role carefully. "I'd been looking for a comedy for 10 years," Foster said. "But I knew that drama is my strong suit and that I wasn't going to get involved in a comedy that wasn't quite there yet with people who didn't know what they were doing. . . .

This was an opportunity to do light, and lightness is a big part of my life." Her gamble turned out to be worthwhile. "I've never been as happy and sane and unwhiny on a film before in my life," she enthused after *Maverick* was finished shooting. "I just said, 'Well, this is not what I do—I'm just going to do whatever you say. And I figure if I'm having a good time it'll be OK."

Her costars were pleasantly surprised at Jodie's ability to adapt to improvised situations. Mel Gibson recalls how the first scene required Foster to step down delicately from a stagecoach. Without warning, the actress performed a hilarious pratfall. "It was so against what she was doing and who she was, it was *funny*," he laughed. James Garner, who had worked with Jodie 20 years earlier on the film *One Little Indian*, claimed that from the start he had been charmed by the youngster. "She had a presence even then—such a little professional; she could do whatever needed to be done. Her attitude and temperament haven't changed," he joked, "she's just gotten better."

Jodie Foster's foray into big-budget, big-studio pictures did not deter her from pursuing her goal of directing her own projects, however. The first Egg Pictures film, *Nell* (1994), the story of a backwoods orphan who speaks her own mysterious language, would prove to her fans and colleagues that Foster had become a powerful force in Hollywood and that, like Nell herself, the newly minted producer had a language and intelligence distinctly her own.

Jodie starred in the 1999 film Anna and the King, *based on a novel about a 19th-century British governess hired to teach the children of the king of Siam. Jodie traveled to Southeast Asia to film the classic East-meets-West tale.*

9

THE MOTHER OF MANY CHILDREN

The qualities that drew Jodie Foster to the character of Nell were the opposite of those she saw in herself. "You have a woman who wears her emotions on the outside. I, personally . . . spend my whole life wearing my emotions on the inside and trying to protect them by sort of cynicism and socialization."

Nell is a young Appalachian woman discovered in a cabin in North Carolina after her mother, who was partially disabled by a stroke, has died. Nell has lived completely isolated from other people; not only does she know nothing of everyday conveniences such as fast food, electricity, and running water, but she also does not speak English. Instead, she has developed her own language that partly mimics the mangled speech of her mother. A psychologist in Charlotte, North Carolina, (Natasha Richardson) hears about Nell, and before long word is out that a scientific wonder has been uncovered, a true "wild child" whom the modern world is eager to dissect. Eventually the local doctor (Liam Neeson) and the psychologist realize that Nell may not be "civilized" in a way that they understand, but she is nevertheless her own person.

What Jodie Foster herself learned while portraying the movie's

Jodie Foster's performance as Nell, a wild young woman who has grown up outside of civilization in the Appalachian Mountains, netted her another Academy Award nomination as Best Actress.

lead character was that it wasn't as difficult as she had believed to be emotionally accessible. "That was the big revelation for me," she said during interviews publicizing the movie. She explained that part of her reluctance to reveal her emotions had evolved as she became a celebrity. "That's part of being a public figure . . . where people say just virtually anything about you, and you do have to build some kind of armor [against it.]"

Reviewers were nearly unanimous in praising *Nell* as yet another in Foster's string of acting successes.

"[Foster] undercuts cliché with a fearless, fierce, beau-tifully attuned performance," declared *Time* reviewer Richard Corliss. Most critics were less generous, how-ever, in appraising her producing skills. Some thought that the story line was overly sentimental; others criti-cized the film because it wasn't as "risky" or "subtle" as they thought a Jodie Foster film should be. By and large, however, the film was an audience pleaser, tak-ing in more than $30 million before Foster was nomi-nated for another Academy Award.

How did Jodie Foster handle being a producer and actress at the same time? One way she managed her double duty was to observe a self-imposed rule: during the hours that the film was shooting, she would function only as an actress. To do otherwise, she believed, would ruin her relationship with her costars and the crew. And because she had been in the position herself, she knew the importance of giving *Nell*'s director, Michael Apted, plenty of leeway. "It's Michael's movie," she explained. "[If] the director feels one way and you feel another way, well you always go with the director."

Jodie Foster was now one of the four highest-paid actresses in America—commanding more than $5 mil-lion per picture—and the only one to have directed box-office successes and to head her own production company. *Entertainment Weekly* dubbed her the Most Powerful Woman in Hollywood. "Foster is attempting what few, if any, Hollywood actresses have ever accom-plished: to become a major player in the film business and [to] do so on her own terms," exclaimed Hilary de Vries of the *Los Angeles Times Magazine*. Noting that nearly all of Jodie Foster's actor/director forerunners were male—Rob Reiner, Ron Howard, Clint Eastwood, and Robert Redford, for example—de Vries pointed out that Foster was one of the rare women who had become a proven director in her own right, without the financial backing or influence of a powerful husband, boyfriend, or male relative.

"This is not a business that is kind to women, but it needs them," Jodie says. "The female pioneers have to be 10 times better than a man. Maybe someday there will be an old-girl network." Still, she says, "I believe in the system. I'm acutely conscious of the business in this town and how I organize my career. . . . You must have self-knowledge and an understanding of your limits."

Yet for all her influence, Foster still describes herself as being "as normal as any American housewife." She still loves spending an afternoon or evening sitting in a dark movie theater with a bucket of popcorn, especially if she's watching a French film. She enjoys cooking, and in her spare time she reads or occasionally watches TV. She does not have an assistant because she considers her household routines—doing laundry, picking up dry cleaning, going grocery shopping—"a great vacation" from her work. She doesn't own a second home, as most celebrities do. She follows an exercise regimen that includes kickboxing. Her most prized possessions are a collection of images by famous photographers and first editions of her favorite literary works.

One would expect her to have a huge, luxurious corner office filled with awards and memorabilia from her films, but she does not. The walls of her modest Sunset Boulevard office are decorated with a favorite photograph of her niece Amanda and several black-and-white photographs taken by friends. Although important business-related items—such as most of her scripts and her Oscars—are at home, Jodie prefers to keep work at her office, separate from her home life.

Still, she insists that she is never more comfortable than when she is on a movie set—and the desire to be there is what drives her. But Jodie Foster's deep need for privacy and normalcy often plays out in the kind of films she chooses to act in and produce. A good example is her second Egg Pictures film, *Home for the Holidays* (1995), the first film involving Jodie Foster in which she did not appear on-screen.

Home for the Holidays is a comedy about the dysfunctional Larson family, seen primarily through the eyes of one of the daughters, Claudia (Holly Hunter). When Claudia travels to Baltimore to spend Thanksgiving with her relatives, we are introduced to her eccentric mother, Adele (Ann Bancroft), her genial father, Henry (Charles Durning), her frenetic gay brother (Robert Downey Jr.), her self-righteous sister (Cynthia Stevenson), and other sundry oddballs.

The attraction for Foster was that the movie flows from several points of view. "The tone shifts all over the place," she said while conducting an interview with Holly Hunter, "and somehow the chaos is managed. But it's still about chaos," about the ways in which family and friends miscommunicate yet manage to find "one singular, beautiful idea that unites them all." Interestingly, Foster sees the three siblings in the film as various

Jodie was back behind the camera for Home for the Holidays, *the second production made by her company, Egg Pictures.* Home for the Holidays *marked the first time that Jodie was involved in a film but did not appear on screen.*

The foremost aspect of Jodie Foster's character in Contact, *Ellie Arroway, "is that she is completely and totally passionate," Foster said in a 1997 interview. "And that's something I was dying to play: somebody that is very involved and very focused on an intellectual process, and that process allows her to fly in ways that feel very loving and emotional."*

aspects of her own personality; in fact, she believes that to be a good director one has to see some part of one-self in every main character and work out resolutions among the characters based on one's experiences.

This philosophy is also the reason Foster prefers to feature brave characters who stand up for themselves despite problems and roadblocks. To those who take Jodie Foster to task for playing victims, she responds, "I always identify with the underdog . . . so I either want to play them or play in films that support them and have something to say about them. There are certain sorts of unconscious paths you choose." Yet she is quick to explain that her characters are not so much victims as people who have been "disenfranchised" by virtue of their upbringing, their looks or actions, their social status, or even the way they think. She believes that she takes on these characters out of a need to "save" or "represent" them.

And yet Foster's characters are by no means helpless. They invariably triumph over their adversity and emerge wiser from their experience. And they never use their "victimhood" as a badge, a means to declare that they are different from others. Such behavior, Jodie believes, is selfish, and it stunts one's development.

Such themes were evident the 1997 film *Contact*, a sci-fi drama based on astronomer Carl Sagan's best-selling novel of the same name. Jodie Foster plays Ellie Arroway, a no-nonsense radio astronomer who yearns for her long-dead father. When she and her crew receive communication from an alien form of life, she agrees to be sent into space to confirm it, despite ridicule from many sides. While there, she experiences what she believes is a conversation with her father. "In some ways, [this character] is a prodigy," Foster says. "If you're a prodigy, that means . . . you have to [expect] that everybody's going to laugh at you. Nobody's going to have any respect for you. And you have to believe consistently and independently that what you're going for is more important."

To prepare for her role, Foster spent months reading what she called the "baby books" of science—basic, informative works that brought her up to speed to play a highly trained astronomer who rattles off scientific jargon that the actress herself doesn't completely comprehend. Foster also had to acquaint herself for the first time with sophisticated special effects. During scenes in which audience-thrilling effects occur, the actors must deliver their performance in front of a blank blue screen. "It's really hard," she said of the adjustment. "You keep trying to make things spontaneous and real, but in a special-effects scene, everything's dead set against [that effort] because there's nothing *there*."

Though Foster once described Arroway as annoyingly zealous, she admires the character's single-minded efforts to communicate with a being greater than herself. This spiritual aspect of the film was derived directly from Sagan himself, with whom Foster spent many hours (Sagan died seven months before the picture was released). "Carl was probably the most romantic person I've ever met," Foster said in 1997. "He had this extraordinary passion . . . for [a field] that's usually considered very dry. He'd take the genuine, intellectual experience and lift it up and say, . . . 'How could you live without this?' And I hope we bring a little bit of that feeling to this movie."

Most critics agreed that the picture had done just that. *E! Online* called the movie "a thinking man's space epic—with a thinking woman as the central character," and Foster earned a Golden Globe nomination for her performance. Many reviewers commented on the themes of single parenthood and abandonment, which are components of Ellie Arroway's personality. Foster admits that these subjects are among the biggest draws for her, part of a motif that seems to run through nearly all of her films, from *The Little Girl Who Lives Down the Lane* to *Contact*.

Family relationships were very much on Jodie Foster's mind in 1997. That year her brother Buddy published *Foster Child*, an unauthorized biography of Jodie that delved into the personal lives of every member of the family. The book included bombshells such as his mother's alleged lesbian affairs and speculation about Jodie's sexuality. Always a fiercely private person, Jodie publicly attacked her brother, calling the book a "cheap cry for attention and money." She stated that she had seen Buddy only a few times in the previous 20 years and that the book consisted merely of "hazy recollections, fantasies, and borrowed press excerpts." Mostly, she said, she felt sorry for her mother, who

"struggl[ed] to raise four children on her own with dignity and strength of character." Buddy, a construction
worker and recovered substance abuser, expressed sur-
prise that Jodie would even acknowledge his book, yet
he insisted that he had the right to tell "his" story.
"This is my life, too," he declared. The standoff
between the siblings continues today.

Parenthood seemed to be the theme for Jodie that
year. In March 1998 she told *New York Post* columnist
Liz Smith that she was expecting a baby, due the following September. Despite prodding by the media,
Jodie refused to name the father or the method by
which she had become pregnant. The news pleasantly
surprised even some of her close friends. "I had no idea
this was on her mind," director Michael Apted said.
"Whenever we talked it was about work." Best pal
Randy Stone, who produced *Little Man Tate*, joked
that Jodie had only two challenges left. "I guess she
could be president if she wanted to," he said, "but since
politics [don't interest her,] it is the most natural thing
in the world that she will be a mother. She's a kind and
generous human being. She's a great listener. This kid
is very lucky." Foster insisted that she intended to raise
her child alone, just as her mother had, and that she
hoped to bring the same kind of respect and admiration
to her relationship with her child that she herself had
with Brandy.

In a case of art imitating life, during her pregnancy
Jodie began coproducing a Showtime TV movie called
The Baby Dance, about the struggle for custody
between one baby's birth parents and adoptive parents.
"Nobody's a hero or a villain [in the movie]," she said.
"I like movies about . . . the things we do to each other
and why we do them." The film was scheduled to debut
on August 23.

On July 20, six days after Jodie had appeared at a
press conference to publicize the movie, Charles Foster
was born two months prematurely. Jodie's publicist

declared the new mother "happy as a lark" and announced that Jodie intended to take a year off to spend time with her son. Jodie's next project, she said in an interview the following month, would be to direct a 1930s period piece called *Flora Plum*, starring Claire Danes. But by the end of 1998 Foster was declaring parenthood "the biggest adventure of my life."

"I thought that raising a child was going to be a little bit of science—that you just do A, B, and C and that's it. But it's really an art form," she said. "It's far more artistic than anything I've ever done." Around the same time, rumors emerged from Hollywood that the actress was negotiating for a role that would make her one of the two highest-paid actresses in America. Fox 2000 was apparently offering her $15 million to costar in *Anna and the King*, a remake of the 1946 film *Anna and the King of Siam* (based on a novel of the same name), which had inspired the long-running Broadway musical and 1956 movie, both titled *The King and I*. The rumors turned out to be fact: in December 1998 Foster traveled with her five-month-old son to Thailand (formerly Siam), where shooting for the film was scheduled to begin in January.

By February 1999, however, the studio had relocated the set. The Thai government and the country's film board had protested the portrayal of the historical 19th-century king (the 1956 film *The King and I* is still banned in Thailand). Despite attempts to rewrite the script and soften the character, the Thai Film Board was not mollified, so the cast and crew moved to Malaysia. Despite the initial delays, the movie was filmed without incident and premiered during the 1999 holiday season.

Anna and the King tells the story of King Mongkut (played by Chow Yun-Fat), who hires a British governess to teach his 58 children and bring them into the 20th century. After traveling to Siam alone with her young son, Anna discovers that the job is more difficult than she imagined in a country where tradition is trea-

While Jodie Foster has become one of the most powerful women in Hollywood today, she is dividing her time between her career and raising her young son Charles.

sured above all else. But she also learns that the preju-dices she has held toward the king—and he toward her—are unjustified. The movie allowed Foster to por-tray another strong but emotionally accessible charac-ter. "I . . . don't think I'm a very emotional or brave person, but I attempt to play characters that are," she once said.

Those who know Jodie Foster—and even those who have only seen her on-screen—would probably disagree with her assessment of her own courage. Throughout her career, the very public figure has fought to maintain a private, normal life filled with day-to-day routines and commitments. At the same time she has climbed to the top of the Hollywood ladder—a notoriously difficult achievement for any woman, but especially remarkable for one who has survived the perilous transition from child celebrity to well-adjusted adult. In fact, nearly all of the main characters Jodie Foster has portrayed, and many of those in films she has directed and produced, exhibit the same touch of the heroic—the person who fights both personal and public demons to reach a worthy goal, and who ultimately learns that everything one has ever known about the world and oneself has changed in the process.

"The great anomaly of Foster's career is that she's risen to the top as neither a seductive beauty nor an unbeautiful character actor," Michael Schnayerson wrote in *Vanity Fair* in 1994. "Instead, from the street-tough daughter in *Alice Doesn't Live Here Anymore* and the young prostitute of *Taxi Driver* . . . to her Oscar-winning performances in *The Accused* and *The Silence of the Lambs*, Foster has radiated an outward strength and inner vulnerability. . . . What she becomes, by quelling her fears and confronting her enemies, is something no other American actress of our time has embodied with such consistency and aplomb: a hero."

In late December 1999, Jodie Foster announced that, despite high expectations, she would not reprise her role as Clarice Starling in the sequel to *The Silence of the Lambs*, based on Thomas Harris's best-selling novel *Hannibal*. She decided instead to begin filming *Flora Plum* after learning that Claire Danes (who is attending Yale University) would take a year off from college to work on the picture. Foster is also planning to produce and star in a film—which she calls a "cautionary tale"—about Leni Riefenstahl, an internationally acclaimed photographer who earned lasting infamy for her 1934 Nazi Party documentary *Triumph of the*

Will. Other reports predict that she will also join *Maverick* costar Mel Gibson in a movie about a husband-and-wife bounty-hunting team. Whatever projects she takes on, Jodie Foster intends to keep striving for excellence, both in her professional life and in her private life with her son, Charlie.

In a 1998 press conference Jodie Foster was asked whether she saw parallels between filmmaking and parenthood. "You know," she answered thoughtfully, "you walk onto the set and you want to be a combination of discipline, knowing where you're heading, and . . . being a good leader. But at the same time, you need to let people know that they're free and that they can fly and that no matter what they do, no matter how dumb it looks, you're still going to have a big smile on your face and say, 'That was a great try.'"

"To me," Jodie Foster concluded, "that's parenting."

1962   Alicia Christian "Jodie" Foster born November 19, the fourth child of separated parents, Evelyn "Brandy" Foster and Lucius Fisher Foster III

1963   Brandy Foster, now divorced, moves with her four children to the home of Josephine Hill ("Aunt Jo")

1965   The Fosters move into their own home; Jodie lands the role of the Coppertone baby on a TV commercial, winning out over older brother Lucius IV ("Buddy"), who also auditioned for the part

1969   Appears in an episode of the TV series *Mayberry R.F.D.*

1970–73   Appears in a number of TV series, including *The Courtship of Eddie's Father*, *My Three Sons*, *Bonanza*, and *Gunsmoke*; also appears in an Emmy Award–winning ABC *Afterschool Special*

1972   Earns the title role in the television series, *My Sister Hank* (only the pilot episode is aired); lands her first movie role as the lead in Disney's *Napoleon and Samantha* and is mauled by a lion during filming; appears in *Kansas City Bomber*; enrolls at Le Lycée Français de Los Angeles, an exclusive private school

1973   Stars as Becky Thatcher in musical film version of *Tom Sawyer*; appears with James Garner in *One Little Indian*

1974   Stars in TV version of *Paper Moon*; costars in *Alice Doesn't Live Here Anymore*

1976   Earns Academy Award nomination and National Society of Film Critics Best Supporting Actress award for her role in *Taxi Driver*; appears in *Echoes of a Summer*; stars in *The Little Girl Who Lives Down the Lane* and *Bugsy Malone*, which wins Best Film at the Cannes Film Festival

1977   Films Disney movies *Freaky Friday* and *Candleshoe* (released in 1978); travels to Europe to film *Moi, Fleur Bleue* and *Il Casotto*; is nominated for a Golden Globe Award (Best Motion Picture Actress in a Musical or Comedy) for her performance in *Freaky Friday*; wins four British Academy Awards: Best Newcomer and Best Supporting Actress for both *Bugsy Malone* and *Taxi Driver*

1980   Graduates as valedictorian from Le Lycée Français de Los Angeles; appears in *Carny* and *Foxes*; enrolls at Yale University

1981–82   Wins Screen Artists Guild Award for her performance in *Foxes*; John Hinckley Jr. attempts to assassinate President Ronald Reagan, claiming he did so to impress Foster. Edward Richardson is arrested after sending Foster a threatening letter. Foster attempts to come to terms with the events by publishing an article in *Esquire* magazine entitled "Why Me?"

1982–3　Appears in *O'Hara's Wife*, a made-for-TV movie; costars with Peter O'Toole in *Svengali*

1984　Costars in *The Hotel New Hampshire*, *Le Sang des Autres* (*The Blood of Others*), and *Mesmerized*, for which she is credited as a coproducer

1985　Graduates magna cum laude from Yale University with a B.A. in African-American literature

1987　Costars in *Siesta*

1988　Appears in *Five Corners*, for which she receives an Independent Spirit Award; appears in *Stealing Home*; wins Academy Award for Best Actress, Golden Globe Award for Best Actress in a Drama, and a National Board of Review Award for Best Actress for her performance in *The Accused*

1989　Appears in *Backtrack* (never released in American theaters)

1991　Directs and costars in *Little Man Tate*; costars with Anthony Hopkins in *The Silence of the Lambs*, for which she wins the Academy Award for Best Actress, the New York Film Critics Circle Award for Best Actress, and the Golden Globe and British Academy Award for Best Actress

1992　Creates her own production company, Egg Pictures; makes a cameo appearance in Woody Allen's *Shadows and Fog*

1993　Costars with Richard Gere in *Sommersby*

1994　Costars with Mel Gibson in *Maverick*; wins the National Association of Theatre Owners' George Eastman Award for her "enormous contribution to the industry as an actress, director, and producer"; produces and stars in *Nell*, the first Egg Pictures film, for which she receives an Academy Award nomination, a Golden Globe nomination for Best Actress, and the Screen Actors Guild Best Actress Award for 1994

1995　Directs *Home for the Holidays*, the second Egg Pictures film

1997　Stars in *Contact*, for which she earns a Golden Globe nomination

1998　Gives birth to a son, Charles Foster, on July 20; becomes the highest-ranking woman among *Premiere* magazine's 100 Most Powerful People; coproduces the Showtime movie *The Baby Dance*, which receives an Emmy nomination for Outstanding Made-for-TV Movie

1999　Is honored by American Cinematheque for career achievement; is named the third most bankable Hollywood actress in the *Hollywood Reporter*'s annual survey of international filmmakers; costars in *Anna and the King*

2000　Produces *Flora Plum*

FILMOGRAPHY

Five Corners, 1988.

The Accused, 1988.

Stealing Home, 1988.

Backtrack, 1989.

Little Man Tate (actor/director), 1991.

The Silence of the Lambs, 1991.

Shadows and Fog (cameo appearance), 1992.

Sommersby, 1993.

It Was a Wonderful Life (voice), 1993.

Maverick, 1994.

Nell (actor/producer), 1994.

Home for the Holidays (producer/director), 1995.

Contact, 1997.

Anna and the King, 1999.

Flora Plum (producer/director), 2000.

FURTHER READING

Chunovic, Louis. *Jodie: A Biography*. Chicago: Contemporary Books, 1995.

Cook, Pam, and Philip Dodd, eds. *Women and Film: A Sight and Sound Reader*. Philadelphia: Temple University Press, 1993.

Corliss, Richard. "A Screen Gem Turns Director." *Time* 138 (14 October 1991): 68–72.

de Vries, Hilary. "Command Performance." *Los Angeles Times Magazine*, 11 December 1994.

Foster, Jodie. "Jodie Foster Talks About Her New Film" [Nell]. Interview by Noah Adams. *All Things Considered*. National Public Radio, 2 December 1994.

———. "Jodie Foster Talks About Her New Movie Contact and Her Life." Interview by Larry King. *Larry King Live*. CNN, 17 July 1997.

———. "Search for Spirituality." Interview by Elizabeth Vargas and Charles Gibson. *Good Morning America*. ABC, 7 July 1997.

———. "Why Me?" *Esquire* 98 (December 1982): 101–2.

Kennedy, Philippa. *Jodie Foster: A Life on Screen*. New York: Birch Lane Press, 1996.

Smolen, Diane. *The Films of Jodie Foster*. New York: Carol Publishing Group, 1996.

INDEX

PICTURE CREDITS

Therese De Angelis received an M.A. in English literature from Villanova University. She was a contributing editor for Chelsea House's *The Black Muslims* and *Rosie O'Donnell*, as well as for the WOMEN WRITERS OF ENGLISH and MODERN CRITICAL INTERPRETATIONS series. She is also the author of several books for young adults, including *Native Americans and the Spanish* and *Louis Farrakhan*, and is coauthor of *Marijuana* in Chelsea House's JUNIOR DRUG AWARENESS series.

Matina S. Horner was president of Radcliffe College and associate professor of psychology and social relations at Harvard University. She is best known for her studies of women's motivation, achievement, and personality development. Dr. Horner has served on several national boards and advisory councils, including those of the National Science Foundation, Time Inc., and the Women's Research and Education Institute. She earned her B.A. from Bryn Mawr College and her Ph.D. from the University of Michigan, and holds honorary degrees from many colleges and universities, including Mount Holyoke, Smith, Tufts, and the University of Pennsylvania.